to Rick

Richard O Snelson

Lunker

Bass Fishin', Country Music and Side-splitting Ozark Humor. Set in Branson, Mo.

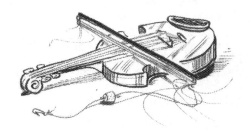

by
Richard O. Snelson

Illustrations by Tom Goldsmith
Canadian wildlife artist
www.timberdoodles.com

Copyright © 2006 by Richard O. Snelson

ISBN 0-7414-3290-0

Illustrations by Tom Goldsmith

Cover Design by J. Allen Williams

Edited by Marna Poole

Published by:

PUBLISHING.COM

1094 New DeHaven Street, Suite 100
West Conshohocken, PA 19428-2713
Info@buybooksontheweb.com
www.buybooksontheweb.com
Toll-free (877) BUY BOOK
Local Phone (610) 941-9999
Fax (610) 941-9959

Printed in the United States of America

Printed on Recycled Paper

Published June 2006

Table of Contents

Introduction

I have woven this story with country music, fishing, and a humorous twist of tales that take place in laidback Ozark country.

Half the fun of writing this story of John "Lunker" Johnson, the pro bass fisherman, and his little friend Red was in my meeting and visiting with the country music show folks of Branson, Missouri. Invitations to sit in on the practice sessions and meet the singers and musicians provided the background and fine down-home feeling that I wanted this book to have.

I invite you to follow along as Lunker and his buddy Red do their best to keep the Chicago "hoods" from bringing gambling and other vices to the warm, homespun, Missouri town of Branson. I hope you enjoy reading it as much as I did writing it for you. This book is dedicated to all who have ever wet a line in anticipation of catching a "lunker bass."

My thanks to my son, Rick Snelson Jr., and Andre' Brunnert for the storyline, and to Woody P. Snow for the screenplay version of Lunker.

Rich Snelson

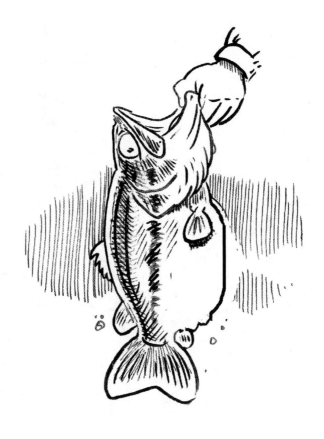

"Red"

1

Lunker's New Buddy

Before I tell you the story of how I came to be friends with John "Lunker" Johnson, let me introduce myself. I'm a short, furry critter with a brown back and a flaming orange belly and tail. Folks holler, "There goes Red!" when they see me scamper by.

It was an Indian summer day in the Ozarks, not far from Branson...

Spread-eagled on the hickory tree limb, I watched the flight of the flashing fishing lure. With each cast the spinner blade got closer and closer to my ambush. The fisherman stood braced against the pedestal on the front deck of the bass boat as he trolled under the overhanging limbs along the bank. I had watched this fellow in action before, bringing up a hiding bass to suck in the lure, just as it hit the surface.

He was hard to miss with his sandy blond hair combed back over his sun-baked ears and face. His fishing outfit always was the same—tan shirt and pants. The shirt had an emblem of a large striking bass sewn above the pocket. The man's name, "Lunker," was stitched there too.

The spinner whooshed toward my hickory tree limb. I was ready. I couldn't resist trying to swipe a shiny new "hot" lure for my collection. It took only a small hop on the branch to snag the lure. He glanced up but didn't see me hunkered down on the limb. As he whipped the rod to free the lure there came a mighty yank that caught me by surprise. It wasn't a pretty sight, my pausing there in mid-air, about to become a flying squirrel. Whoa! Down I went, right on his back. Holy jumping acorns! This guy was a giant of a man!

His long arms thrashed as he tried to knock the demon off his back. Instead, he knocked his rod and reel overboard. He could really cuss! I leapt for my life and ran along the edge of the boat, jumping to the top of the towering black motor.

I stood tall, whipping my tail, as the hairs on my back rose like a thousand quills. I aimed at his face and spit what was left of a hickory nut at his nose. The look in his eyes said "Only one of us is going to leave this boat alive." He grabbed a paddle and swung. Wham! That hurt! Now I had a hunk of hair out of my tail and an ugly bend right in the middle of it. That bend would never come out.

Mom's teaching flashed to my mind: "Act like you're possessed by the devil when cornered." So I charged. I grabbed the man's leg, scratching and clawing up his side. His eyes bulged like two big hickory nuts. I jumped for the tree. He staggered, tripped over the paddle, and fell overboard. I dangled from the limb, watching as he came up spitting water. He swam to the bank and crawled to his feet, stomping and mumbling under his breath.

"Darned squirrel. Why in the heck did you have to do that?"

I raced to the far side of the tree and peeked back at the crazy man talking to a squirrel.

"Look what you've done! Best rod at the bottom of the lake, boat heading down the lake, and I'm sitting here soaking wet. Got a wedding to go to. Nobody is going to believe me when I tell them a squirrel knocked me out of my boat. You know, Red, all I ever wanted to do was marry Millie Como and be the best bass fisherman in the world. That's why I'm out here practicing, on my wedding day. I'm going to set the world bass tournament record. Catch twenty-four pounds more and I've got it. Gotta get to a road, quick."

Lunker stared at the steep bluff that bordered the south side of the lake, looking for a path to the top.

He took a deep breath and started up through the brush and trees. His feet dug at the dirt and loose rocks as he struggled toward a sheer rock face, half-way up the bluff. He moved up, hand over hand, rock to rock, tree to tree, and finally paused to catch his breath. He rested with his foot braced against a small tree. Again, up he climbed toward the ledge below the rock face. With only a foot to go, he reached with one hand to grip the edge.

The rocks under his feet broke loose. He tore down the hill; his butt hit the rocks as he bounced back and forth between standing and sitting. His fingers scraped the bark of the trees as he ricocheted off their sides. He was going about as fast as I've ever seen a man move, when he hit the water and disappeared. It took forever before he shot up, spitting water and wiping his eyes.

"Don't know what I'm going to do after I get to that ledge, Red. The cliff is straight up. Be easy for a squirrel. Not for me. Hope somebody's fishing; that's going to be the only way I get off this bank."

A good bit of the afternoon passed as he tried again and again to climb the steep cliff. I watched as bass boats raced along the far side of the lake. Lunker waved his arms and shouted, trying to get their attention. No one noticed. He sat a bit and then paced

6

back and forth along the narrow bank.

"She's the best thing that ever came along in my life. Been putting up with my being late—can't remember for how long. This'll be the last minnow in the bucket for me."

The sun was rushing to find the horizon when a boat finally came up our side of the lake. Well, maybe it was a boat. As it got closer, I saw it was eight aluminum canoes tied to together with rusty bailing wire. The canoes looked like they had been over some really bad white-water rapids. A dozen warped boards were strapped across the top, with a tiny motor chugging on the back. One man sat on the boards, working on his fishing pole; the other rocked in an old gray chair, fooling with something I couldn't make out. The wind was behind them, blowing right up my nose.

"What's that smell?" Lunker asked. "Smells like a pig pen."

The motor burped and popped, sounding like it would quit at any moment. It kept coming. I could hear them talking.

"Your mama told you to wash that stink out of them overalls before you come home, Junior," said the tall skinny one, rocking in the chair.

"How am I gonna wash them overalls, Roy? I don't have nuthin' else to wear."

"Jump in the lake with some of Mama's homemade lye soap and paddle your fat self around," said Roy, flapping his arms like a beached carp.

"Can't do that. Can't swim. Besides, it ain't my fault they stink," said Junior, as he sniffed the top of his overalls.

"Dang nab it, Junior! I told you that sow and all them pigs would never house break."

I froze when I spotted the squirrel rifle braced against the rocking chair. It was then that I recognized the "oldboys." Squirrel killers! I prayed Lunker would keep still about our run-in.

"Over yonder, Junior! Fellow waving at us. I think he wants us to stop."

"You know our mama said to never pick up no hitchhikers," said Junior, shaking his head.

"That's on the road, stupid. Turn on over there."

As the short fat dude steered the boat toward the bank, the skinny one stood up from his rocker, tugged at his bibs, and scratched his dirty bare chest. I re-member tales from the other squirrels of how he's the one to watch out for. He'd throw rocks behind the tree to spook a squirrel hiding there. Young ones would scurry away from the crashing rock sound and get shot dead, right on the spot.

"Howdy, boys."

"Howdy, mister." Roy's two front teeth stuck way out when he smiled. "Ain't you that Lunker pro fishing man from over at the dock?"

"Reckon so. You the Taneys from over at Skunk Creek Cove?"

From a squirrel's point of view, they should have stayed in Skunk Creek Cove with all their stinking relatives.

"We is. I mean, we are those. Yes, sir, we are the brothers Taney. I'm Roy; this here is Junior. He's my forty-eight-year-old kid brother."

"I need a big favor, boys. I'm going to miss my wed-ding if I don't get over to the boat ramp at the Table Rock Dam, quick."

"We'll take you over there in our speedboat," said

Roy.

Lunker climbed on the rickety "speedboat" and watched Junior wrap the rope around the top of the tiny motor. It took about a dozen yanks before the motor made a sound. It finally popped and belched to a start; off they headed across the wide lake. I swished my tail in relief.

They got about fifty tree limbs away when the motor missed a bunch of licks. It kept going and made it to the middle of the lake before its last lick. It burped twice, belched a cloud of gray smoke, and ground to a halt.

"Grab somethin'. Paddle, Junior," Roy ordered.

"Got nuthin' but fishin' poles, Roy."

I wanted to shout, "Use your squirrel rifle! Paddle with it, you idiots!" Maybe they would drop it, and it would sink to the bottom of the lake. I climbed higher in the tree.

"I'm sorry you have to hold your nose, Mr. Lunker. Junior stinks real bad. Tell him how come, Junior."

"Roy sent me to the pound to get a good coon dog. I came back with a tracking sow pig instead, 'cause a man there sold it to me. Said, 'when the dog gets old you still have to feed him, you could eat the pig.'"

Lunker shook his head and sat with his face buried in his hands. They sat, drifting in the middle of the lake. Lunker must have been desperate, 'cause he stood up and ripped a board from the top of the canoe boat and tried to paddle with it. It was slow—way too slow. Lunker was going to be late for his wedding!

"Mr. Lunker, what kind of bait you gonna use in the big Lilly Bean Fishin' Tournament?" Roy asked.

"I'm sorry, boys. Can't stay to talk. I'm going to swim for it. Tell you what—when you get her going again, how 'bout rounding up my bass boat and towing it over to the marina? I'll make it up to you later. We'll head up to Springfield; get some lures at the Bass Fishing Shop up there."

Lunker tied his shoes together, looped them around his neck and dove into the lake. As he swam for the far shore, I climbed to the tiptop of the tree to watch. It would be a long swim.

2

I'll Know It's Over

Red knew it was late and that John Lunker Johnson had missed his wedding. He watched as Lunker finally reached the other side of the lake and climbed out of the water. Lunker struggled behind the wheel of his Suburban, started the engine, and headed straight for Millie's house. He would have a lot of explaining to do to get out of the mess he was in.

Millie always left a light on in the living room, but tonight the house was pitch-black dark. She was gone. Lunker sat in the driveway, thinking where she might be. His best hope for finding her tonight would be their best friends, Cal and Figgy Willis. He backed out of the drive and headed for the Willises'.

The headlights of the Suburban lit the rundown house and yard full of toys as Lunker turned into the driveway. The Willises' big Chow dog came around the house, barked, and stopped when he recognized the Suburban. The dog sat on his haunches, waiting for Lunker to give him the usual ear scratching.

"Hello, boy. Have you seen my Millie tonight?" He rubbed the dog's ear.

"Sorry, Lunker. She ain't your Millie any longer."

"You sitting up on the porch in the dark, Figgy?"

"After what happened at church today...well, I felt like sitting in the dark, with no men around."

"I'm sorry. Really, I am, but—"

"Don't try to explain what happened. Millie was worried sick about you. I knew you had gone and done something stupid. I've quit caring, Lunker."

"Where is she, Figgy? I've got to explain."

"Why should I tell you? You've hurt her enough for one lifetime."

"I love her, really love her, Figgy."

"Have an oddball way of showing it, mister. Leaving her standing at the altar with everybody watching."

"But, Figgy, you don't—"

"Just shut the heck up, Lunker."

Lunker knew he would find Millie a lot quicker with Figgy's help. He climbed the steps and sat down beside her. He'd shut up; let nature's love calls work on the will of a woman. Bullfrogs were booming to their mates in the pond. A peepers' chorus of thousands sang out in nature's lust.

Each whip-poor-will's call was echoed in stereo by its mate. Out on the pond, the reflection of the orange harvest moon slowly turned silver, enough to cause any woman to think of romance, Lunker reasoned. For Figgy, it was enough.

"Oh, dang you, John Lunker Johnson. Look over at the Opry. If you hadn't been spending so much time out on that lake, you'd know they're having the big twenty-fifth anniversary celebration. All of the local Branson folks are there tonight."

"Thanks, Figgy. I owe you one," Lunker said, as he jumped to his feet.

"Naw, Lunker, you owe Cal. Not me. He said you would come looking for her. If he weren't your best friend... well! Told me to tell you."

Lunker spun out of the driveway and headed for Branson's 76 Country Music Row. The Suburban roared into town, going more than a little over the speed limit. The bright, colorful lights of the Branson theaters rolled across the windshield as Lunker sped by. He would have missed the red one flashing behind him if it hadn't been for the siren. He pulled over and dropped his head on the steering wheel, waiting for the knock on the car window. That came quickly enough in the form of a uniform wrapped tightly around a red-headed, six-foot-tall deputy sheriff named Judy Campbell.

"Well, hello, John. Looks like you're in a big hurry to find the nightlife in Branson."

Judy leaned way over, with her elbow inside Lunker's car window.

"Judy."

"Heard a rumor that you called off the wedding."

Lunker always had something to say. But right about now, he sat quietly, biting his lip. Judy reached in the window and pushed a piece of paper against the palm of his hand.

"If you're feeling lonely tonight, here's my new number. I'm done at eleven. Oh, by the way, slow down— when you're driving. Bye, hon," Judy purred.

Lunker rubbed his forehead as Judy turned off the flashing red lights and pulled the patrol car around him. He thought she had given up on him a long time ago. Guess not, Lunker.

The Opry parking lot was packed, but John Lunker Johnson, the bass fishing pro, got special treatment in Branson. All the folks knew and liked him. He pulled right up to the back door, shook hands with the security guard, and walked down the steps to the backstage area to look for Millie. He stopped to listen.

The morning sunrise won't seem the same
now that it's hard to speak your name.
When evening comes and you're not here
I'll know it's over, really over,
and someday, someway—I'll try not to care.

Lunker didn't catch all the words of the song. If he had, he might have turned and walked back out the stage door. Millie was wrapped in the stage curtains, watching the show. She must have felt him looking at her because she turned suddenly. Her look of surprise quickly became a blazing stare that burned Lunker's face. She spun out of the curtain and raced at him, peppering his chest with both fists.

"Damn you, Lunker Johnson! Damn you! Don't you say

a word, John Lunker Johnson. If you say one word, I'll go out there on that stage and tell everybody in Branson what you did today."

"Millie..."

"That's it! You said it! I'm going out there."

The singer was on the last verse when Millie reached center stage.

"I know it's over, really over—"

"Give me that mike!" She grabbed it from the startled singer. The band froze on a G chord that ended in a squeak.

"Drum roll, please," Millie demanded. "Mr. Mayor and honored citizens of the city of Branson. Most of you know me; I'm Millie Como; Today your favorite big-time bass-kissin' professional fisherman was supposed to marry me. Well, the little boy was too busy, out practicing for the farting Lilly Bean Bass Tournament. Right now, he's standing backstage looking like a red-faced baboon. Why don't you all give him a big hand, and maybe he'll come out and tell us why he couldn't make it to his own wedding."

The crowd whistled, clapped their hands, and started

a yelling tizzy. The floor shook as a thousand feet stomped to each shout.

"Lunker!" "Lunker!" "Lunker!"

Lunker was sweating now! He stumbled forward as someone from behind the curtain pushed him onto the stage. He caught himself and held up his hand in a puny wave to the crowd.

"Well, here's the big guy now. Step right up, if you can walk, Mr. John Lunker Johnson. Looks like you just climbed out of your mother's washing machine. Gonna tell all the folks why you missed coming to your wedding?" Millie shoved the mike into Lunker's chest.

He cleared the frogs from his throat. "First, let me say..."

"Boo! Boo! Hiss! Hiss!"

The crowd wanted to be part of the real-life melodrama they were watching on the stage.

"I just want to say...I love you, Millie Como," said Lunker, turning toward Millie.

"Hey, bud. Missing your wedding is a funny way of showing it!" someone shouted.

"It's true, I was fishing earlier. I had an accident, and, well, the accident made me late."

"What kind of accident? What kind of accident did you have?"

"It was a trick...well, a squirrel—oh, hell, never mind. I'm sorry it happened. I do love Millie Como."

Lunker's chin dropped as he handed the mike to Millie and left the stage. The crowd's booing and hissing got louder. Pausing at the stage door, he looked back. The woman he loved wasn't watching. The words of the song echoed in his mind.

When evening comes and you're not here
I'll know it's over, really over.

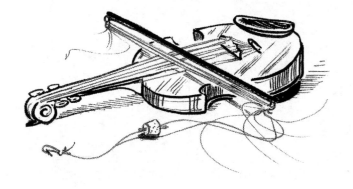

"The Eyes of Texas are Upon You."

3

The Snapping Turtle

The next morning I was traveling along my favorite tree route, the south shore of the lake. It's there that I search for the special sweet hickory nuts my mom loves so much. Bass boats were streaking up and down the lake from one cove to another, checking out their favorite bass hidey-holes. I knew they were practicing for the Lilly Bean Bass Tournament.

I'm sure glad they don't practice for squirrel hunting. I'd hate to think that some idiot would shoot me with a 12-gauge for practice. I was in hopes that we could get hunters to practice "catch and release" for squirrels, like Lunker does for bass.

I hid in the top of a pine tree and watched as the metallic red, white, and blue Star of Texas bass boat glided quietly into the waters of the secluded fishing spot. I knew right away it was Kochi Miyako, the Branson music star. His glittering blue jacket was so bright it made me blink. Bill Fox-Trot, his personal fishing guide, steered the boat as Kochi got his gear ready.

As the boat coasted to a stop, Kochi took out a silver fiddle, put it to his cheek, and let rip ten bars of *The Eyes of Texas Are Upon You.* Then he bowed toward the hiding bass and exchanged the fiddle for his silver rod and reel. Then he reached under the seat for a case marked "Secret—Experimental" and took out his newest invention, the Glug-a-Plug.

"You show me where to throw Glug-a-Plug so we get big bass, and I beat Mr. Big Guy Fisherman 'Lunker' Johnson."

"Look, Mr. Miyako, why don't you try a watermelon-salted lizard back in those fallen trees? I don't think the Glug-a-Plug will ever catch fish," said Bill Fox-Trot.

"Please, remain quiet. Must try now. Computer say lure catch fish every cast." Kochi carefully adjusted the settings on his diamond-studded reel.

"Well, if that thing catches fish, I'll eat 'em raw."

"Prepare for lots of sushi, Foxstep."

"Fox-Trot. Fox-Trot."

As Kochi swung the Glug-a-Plug over the edge of the boat, a bass leaped from the water, grabbing it in midair.

"This is it!" Kochi yelled, "I've invented the perfect lure. It catches a fish each time I throw. I hope you plenty hungry, Mr. Foxtrod."

"Fox-Trot, Mr. Miyako. He's only a little fellow. Toss him back. Please?"

"OK, little fishy. You only measure nine inches. I catch your big brother next." Kochi carefully dropped the bass back into the lake.

Kochi whipped the lure toward the back of the cove. Glug. Glug. A strike!

"This is it! I catch the big guy now."

I couldn't believe my little rodent eyes. He caught a bass each time he tossed the secret lure—more than twenty bass before he stopped casting. I'd bet a bag of roasted Jimmy Carter peanuts that Kochi was sure he would win the big Lilly Bean Bass Tournament trophy.

"Mr. Miyako, something is wrong. All the bass are only nine inches long."

"Mr. Foxwox, please shut up. I make you eat lots of sushi. We must go back to secret laboratory now to work more on experimental Glug-a-Plug. Computer will fix problem. Hurry, please." Kochi quickly stowed his rod and hurried for his seat across from Bill.

The Taney brothers were coming around the corner in their canoe boat as Kochi's boat roared out of the cove. Roy and Junior both grabbed for the large crate sitting on the pitching deck.

"Dang city slickers. Can't go out on the water no more without gettin' run over. Start workin' on that electric generator gizmo, Junior. We've got to shock us some big bass. Tie 'em up; hide 'em for the tournament day. What you do with the instruction book?"

"I used it."

"You what?" asked Roy, with a look of complete surprise on his face.

"I used it. I took it up in the woods with me the last time we stopped."

"Why you do that?" Roy shook his head.

"'Cause we didn't have no more seers and rowbucks. That's why. Can't read no how."

"Momma told you to quit wastin' paper, and for us to use corncobs instead. Crank up that thing and stick them prods in the water, Junior. Let's get us some big bass."

"Here goes, Roy. Listen to that thing whine. I bet it's making a jillion jolts."

"It's 'volts,' not 'jolts,' you dummy. Stick the prods in."

"Wow, it's workin'. Look at all them minnows coming up. What's that? It looks like a washtub." Junior leaned way over the side of the boat to push on the blob that had just surfaced.

"That a snappin' turtle. Dang, he's big. Floatin' plum upside-down. Volts got him good. Pull him on the boat quick. Mama will make some good soup out of him," said Roy, running his tongue over his lips.

"He's dead, ain't he?" asked Junior before he grabbed the monster turtle by the tail and hoisted him on the canoe boat.

"He ain't dead, only sleepin' from the shock. Paddle on out in the middle of the cove. We got to find where them big bass are hidin'."

"I've been thinkin', Roy," said Junior, as he scratched the top of his head.

"Don't do too much thinkin', Junior. Mama told you it would be better if I did all the thinkin' for both of us."

"I know. But I was wonderin' what we was gonna to do with all that money when we get the Lilly Bean winnin's. We gonna buy us one of them fancy bass boats?"

"Naw. I think we ought to invest that money in stock."

"Roy, you know we ain't got no fence to hold stock."

"Not that kind of stock, stupid. This that kind you get up in New York City."

"I ain't never been to New York, Roy. Ain't never been past the county stool, 'cept when they sent me off to jail for stealin' that old mare."

"Still think you stole a mare? Idiot! That weren't no mare; it was a hot-blooded Arabian stallion. It tried to straddle both of Uncle Jeb's jumpin' mules. Mules liked to kick that poor stallion to death. Jeb never did find one of the mules. Jumped every fence in the county. It ruined the stallion for life—never would go near another four-legged animal. Stop the boat! It's a biggun."

"Look at that bass. It's a lunker bass."

"Don't say Lunker's name, Junior. It might be bad luck."

"I got him. I got him," said Junior, leaning way over the edge of the boat, about to get a much needed bath.

"Watch out; don't fall. Junior!

"Can't swim! Hel...!"

I told you it was bad luck to say 'Lunker.' Junior, you OK? Get back in the boat, Junior."

"Help! Help me quick, Roy."

"Your face looks funny, Junior. I ain't never seen your eyes so wide open. How come all your hairs are standing straight up?"

"Turn off...turn off...them volts, Roy. Dang thing is killin' me dead."

"OK, Junior. I turned it off. Junior, you're floatin' upside-down, just like that snappin' turtle."

Roy pulled Junior onto the deck and slapped him across the back.

"Wake up, Junior. Junior, wake up."

"I'm 'wake, Roy. Let go my toe, Royeeeeeee! You're hurting my toe really bad."

"Oh shoot, Junior. That snapping turtle done gone and woke up."

4

Weapon of Mass Destruction

Buckshot Mel is a red, like me, but he's getting gray around the edges. He's the oldest squirrel in Taney County. Buckshot earned his name from being shot at so many times and living through it. His jagged ears look like they've been trimmed with pinking shears. Missing some teeth, so he has to be careful when he cracks tough acorns.

After a lot of years in the big timber, putting up with the hunters, Buckshot moved into the heart of Branson. Now he spends his days loafing in the city parks and swiping food from the geese along the lakeshore.

He makes a daily tour of the big new houses and estates surrounding the town, checking out the birdfeeders and all the good-looking sunbathing gals.

I was curled up with my tail over my eyes when old Buckshot stuck his head in the knothole. All the fishing lures hanging on the inside of my den chattered when he barked to wake me up. Buckshot stutters when he gets excited, so you can't always tell what's bothering him.

"Red's Pad"

"Wa...wa...wake up, Red. They're hoods! The ones that bought Twin Peaks Estate are bad...bad dudes."

"Buckshot, you've been going to too many of those Mel, Mel, Mel shows."

Buckshot stuttered on and finally finished telling me what was happening. Some big problems had come to Branson. The Taney County folks weren't going to be happy about their new neighbors.

Buckshot had been up at the Twin Peaks Estate, cleaning out the remains of the birdseed left by the previous owners, when he had a run-in with the new owners. He was hanging by one foot over the top of a bird feeder, with only a couple more sunflower seeds left to stuff into his cheeks, when it all started.

This guy—Buckshot thought he was in his forties—with slick black hair and a mustache, came out on the patio. He was wearing a white silk bathrobe with a huge fur collar. Strange fur, stark white with black patches. May have come from an exotic animal. Panda! Buckshot was glad it wasn't squirrel.

This guy yelled for two other fellows, George and Per-rino. They came running from a shiny new helicopter sitting on the lawn. Buckshot thought they had been unloading a bunch of elephant tusks. George, the big one, stood about twenty hands high with shoulders as broad as the rear end of a Clydesdale. His head was as bare as the horse's nose. Perrino, the little guy, had on a black suit and limo driver's cap.

"Yes, boss. What can we get you?" Perrino asked.

"Branson! Branson! Never thought Francis Quantrill would see the sun rise over this hick town again."

"Why did you come back here, boss?" Perrino asked, staring at the ground.

"Are we going to open an office for the Endangered Species Foundation in Branson?" asked George.

"Every newspaper you pick up talks about Branson being a small, family-oriented town without gambling, vice, or corruption. The place is like a new frontier. I smell gold in them thar hills. Besides, I told Millie Como I'd come back for her someday."

"Millie who, boss?" asked Perrino.

"A sweet broad. Going to make her a part of my family."

"We going to put in some gambling boats and girly shows in Branson?" asked Perrino.

"We're going to do that and more. We're going to buy out these hillbilly-owned country music shows and bring in our own talent from Chicago. Open up a couple of Las Vegas-style casinos. Then change the name of this place to Bransin—Sin City of the Midwest."

"How you going to do that, boss? These country jakes won't let us open no casinos here. They got laws."

"Let's say I have a couple of slick tricks up my sleeve. A good part of this town is sitting on land that they took from the Indians. Our lawyers will get it back for the Indians. Won't be hard to get the redskins to lease it to me. I'll build all the casinos I want on the new Indian reservation. Perrino! Shoot that stinking squirrel hanging on the birdfeeder."

Old Buckshot jumped for his life as the birdfeeder exploded. He had been shot at by every kind of shotgun and rifle a man could nightmare up. This gun was different; it was a weapon of mass destruction. He tore across the lawn toward the helicopter as bullets smacked the grass behind him. The men were laughing at his frantic attempt to escape. Buckshot raced past the helicopter.

"Stop shooting, dummy you're going to hit the heli—"

Old Buckshot didn't look back; it would take more than miserable aim to stop him.

5

Branson or Bran-sin ?

Somehow I had to warn my new friend Lunker about the bad news. I set a fast pace along the telephone wires and through the trees to his log home. He'd had a bad night at the Opry, so I was sure he wouldn't be up yet. I jumped onto the windowsill and stared inside. There he was, sprawled across the bed in the same clothes he had worn all day yesterday. I was really glad Lunker liked to fish instead of hunt squirrels; he had fishing trophies all over the house.

Centered above his trophies he had a picture of himself shaking hands with the president of the United States. He must be really proud of that hand shake.

Lunker's picture of Millie lay beside him on the bed. Her dark hair in the photo glistened in a ray of sunlight that streaked through the window, she's a beauty.

I sat, wondering how to tell him about the danger and how the bad guys at Twin Peaks were planning to take over Branson. I couldn't talk to him; everyone knows that squirrels can't talk. There was only one hope. I'd sit on the windowsill and think about what old Buckshot had told me. I'd think real, real hard and maybe...well; we'd have to see. After a long time of real hard thinking, I let go with a lot of racket.

"Get out of here, you noise-bucket squirrel. Can't you see I've had a bad night?"

I sat there on his windowsill, softly barking, waving my bent tail from side to side.

"Oh! It's you. Followed me, huh? Your tail looks pretty bad, Red."

'You ought to know; you bent it, fish-breath.'

"Lost my girl because of that little trick you pulled on me yesterday. Well, I'd probably have lost her any-way. It's not your fault. It's mine. I should have been home, getting ready for the wedding, instead of out fishing. Oh, well, I'm glad you woke me up. I was hav-ing the dumbest dream."

I couldn't visit any longer because a truck was coming up the lane to Lunker's cabin. As it came to a stop I noticed the "Cal Willis's Ramblers" sign on the side. Lunker was depressed and needed a friend who could talk to him. I was glad to see Cal had come by. I jumped to the rafters of the porch and scooted back out of sight.

"You wake yet, John?" Cal yelled as he pounded on the screen door.

"Come on in, Cal. Talk soft; I've got a banger of a headache."

"Boy, that was some show Millie put on at the Opry," Cal said.

"Well, I didn't want to be any part of it, but some jackass pushed me on stage. I'd like to know who did that."

"Could we say it was a friend?" asked Cal, hiding a smile.

"You?"

"Didn't think it could hurt. Broke the ice. Got Millie talking to you again."

"Well, she talked all right. Had to tell the whole town. Let's go sit on the porch, Cal. I want to tell you about a dream."

"You dreaming about Millie?"

"About Millie and how much I love these Ozark hills and all the folks that make this such a good place to live and work. I wish we could slow down time and the way things change. Happens too quick."

"Tell me about your dream, John," said Cal, sitting on the steps beside Lunker.

"It was about change. Bad changes and bad people moving in on Branson and all the good things we have here. Riverboat gambling and the danger to any of us who stand up to oppose it. Something bad is going to happen here, Cal. I saw it all clear in my dream. Then I woke up with the same stupid squirrel chattering in my face. Bent tail and all. Strangest thing—he must have followed me home."

"You still sticking to that squirrel story, John? I know what you mean about changes coming to Branson. The lawsuit filed by those big city lawyers for the Indians—if they win we're in for some real changes."

"How about you, Cal? Ever want to make it big in the country music business? Get out of Branson and head for the lights and recording studios of Nashville?"

"Ah, most of us pickers always have Nashville somewhere in our minds. Nashville has always been a lot more serious about country music than Branson.

Branson's about fun, John."

"Never thought about it that way, Cal."

"We do a lot of pickin' and then throw in the grinnin'. Folks enjoy the homespun feeling of Branson. Think about it this way, John: I have made it big. Have my own band and get to play six nights a week. I can walk down the street without having fans chase me for autographs, and best of all, I'm living in the Ozarks near some of the best fishing there is. I've made it big, John. Made it big."

"Guess I've made it big too. Really love Millie...got to let her know I'm really sorry about what happened."

"Hang in there, buddy boy. She's a good woman and she'll listen when she gets over being so mad at you."

"Talk to her for me, Cal," said Lunker, putting his hand on Cal's shoulder.

"This one's for you to do, pro."

"She may not give me a chance, friend."

"You need some cheering up—I see you got your boat back. Let's go hit on those Table Rock bass."

"Taneys brought the boat back. Had to promise to show them some pro-fishing tricks. If only Junior didn't smell so bad. Real...bad."

I was sitting high in a tree eating a fine Missouri walnut, when Cal and Lunker climbed in the boat and headed out. I knew Lunker didn't feel like wetting a line, but the fresh cool air coming off the water would help wake him up. His dream had told him about the trouble coming to Taney County, and I knew he would know what to do about it. I headed to town. It was time for a squirrel's call to action.

6

The ATF Agent

A couple months back one of the gray squirrels found a flyer on the boat dock about "Ducks Unlimited." I liked the idea so much that I gathered all the local squirrels and formed our own chapter of "Squirrels Forever." We made plans to lobby the government and outlaw squirrel hunting. With no squirrel hunting allowed, we could go back to living in the deep woods without fear of getting our butts shot off.

Now, I needed all the squirrels of Squirrels Forever to help, so I put out the call on that morning for all of the Taney branch of the grays and reds to head for the back forty of The Ozark Fun Land Park. We would have to work together if we were going to run the crooks out of town.

When we finished our plans, all the squirrels were prepared with their best stealth outfits—a hundred spies ready and willing to watch and listen. Off they went to the drumbeat of a big woodpecker. I stayed around headquarters to wait for the reports to come back.

The first to check back in were the gray squirrels from Taney Hollow.

They reported that the brothers Taney had been paid a visit by a government official.

Getting to the Taneys' shack was easy for a squirrel but a chore for any two-legged animal. What was once a dirt lane was overgrown with scrub brush and poison ivy vines hanging from both sides of a narrow raccoon trail. A tangle of wild grape vines and fallen limbs helped to block the way even more. It kept down visitors, so the Taneys never cleared the lane. They always came in the back way, up a little creek that emptied into Table Rock Lake.

The brothers lived with their mom in a one-hundred-year-old dirt-brown log cabin. A sagging porch clung with its last hope to the front of the cabin. The porch's missing boards let light shine through so you could see all the trash heaped underneath. A rooster and two hens were scratching in the trash, looking for scraps of the Taneys' last night's supper. A black cast-iron kettle filled with water coming to a boil hung over a fire in the yard. It was the first of the month and time for Mama Taney to wash her younguns' bedclothes.

Today, the brothers were busy dreaming about winning the Lilly Bean Bass Tournament. They had spent yesterday collecting the best live baits around—crickets, grasshoppers, crawdads, and worms. All the critters that are on the bottom of the food chain. "The food rope," as Junior called it. Four old-fashioned wide-mouth pickle jars sat in a row across the kitchen table. Each jar was crawling full of the bait critters. Roy and Junior were finishing their breakfast of Lilly Beans and cornbread when their mama stormed in from outside.

"Each jar was crawling full of the bait critters."

"You'uns get them pickle jars off the table 'fore tonight. It was dark in here last night and I wanted a pickle. I stuck my hand in one of them jars. It was them snappin' crawdads. My hand came out with a crawdad on each finger. I was so mad I pulled their tails off and ate 'em raw. I'm gonna dump the whole mess in you'uns' bed if they ain't gone tonight."

"We're sorry, Mama. Thems our bait for the big fishin' doin's. Gonna win all that money and buy a big-screen TV and satellite plate. Junior wants to get the Playboy channel," said Roy. "Look, Junior's feedin' the sow at the table again, Mama."

"We ain't never gonna teach them pigs manners if you keep doin' that, Junior. Look at all the little pigs watchin'. Gonna be beggin', just like their mother 'fore you know it. Careful you don't step on one of them little pigs. Sow will take your foot off," said Mama, slapping Junior on the back of the head.

"Ouch! That hurt, Mama."

"She has been right cranky lately," said Roy.

"You mean Mama or the pig?" whispered Junior.

"I heard that, Junior. One of you boys poke up the fire under the outside kettle before leavin' today. I'm gonna have to wash the sheets," said Mama.

"But you just washed them last spring, Mama," said Junior.

"Shut up, Junior, 'fore I slap you again."

It was then that the Alcohol, Tobacco and Firearms agent arrived in Taney Hollow. Things had changed a lot in the way the ATF worked. They were striving to be a softer, kinder, more understanding agency.

The Taneys' little moonshine operation was more of a nuisance, and this agent had been selected to go out and convince the boys to quit shining. He pushed his way through the brush-covered trail, avoiding the poison ivy vines, and crawled over the big trees that had fallen across the way. He walked up the steps and peered in the screen, not noticing the three little pigs stacked against the door. He couldn't see anyone at home so he beat on the door and yelled, "Anyone home?"

The frightened little pigs leaped in the air with a squeal and raced under the kitchen table. Junior's legs caught the table as he fell backward, and flipped it and the pickle jars high into the air. Grasshoppers shot out in a starburst as their jar exploded against the ceiling. Mama was standing with her mouth open when the escaping grasshoppers reached her. She swallowed three before getting her mouth shut. All the crawdads held claws with their neighbors as they fell to the floor. The earthworms got to the floor last and quickly disappeared into the dirt.

The sow charged, making a blood-curdling screech. She didn't slow down a bit as the outline of her head ripped through the screen door. The startled agent leaped off the porch as three hundred pounds of bacon and fury lunged after him. He raced down the narrow trail through the brush and poison ivy vines, heading for his car.

He looked back as the sow vaulted over the last fallen tree trunk; she nearly grabbed his foot as she landed. He broke out of the brush and made a desperate dive toward the car's open window. The sow managed to grab his pant leg, shaking the dangling limb as it hung out the window of the car. The agent's pant leg ripped off at the crotch, and the sow circled the car, ramming her head against the sides and shaking her flag of victory.

"Damn Cujo pig!" the agent screamed.

Back in the house, all the little pigs learned to eat in the kitchen. They lapped up the bottom of the food chain on the kitchen floor. Roy and Junior shoved the pigs away, trying to get back what was left of their bait.

"300 pounds of bacon and fury"

"Who do you reckon was at the door, Roy?"

"Don't know, Junior. Sure did leave in a hurry. Un-friendly sort," added Roy.

Mama was spitting and spewing, trying to get the grasshopper juice out of her mouth. The pot of stew on the kitchen woodstove was a good deal richer in protein from all the fallout it had received. Roy said it was the most uplifting experience he'd ever had. Junior said it could be like a five-ring circus, but he wasn't sure since he could only count to four. Mama said she was damn sure she didn't have no kids, 'cause hers couldn't be as stupid as Roy and Junior. The brothers hid the few baits that were left, out back in the smokehouse.

Down the lane the ATF agent drove off, after he took the Taney brothers' moonshine operation off the nuisance list and moved it to the dangerous and threatening category. He would be back with some help—after the head-to-toe itching from the poison ivy stopped. The Taneys left the shack and headed for Table Rock Lake to meet Lunker and get some tips from a real pro fisherman. I thanked the grays for a good report and climbed higher in the tree to watch the downtown happenings.

Branson motel parking lots were full. Country music

fans couldn't get rooms because of all the fishing folks that had come to Branson, hoping to win the $250,000 Lilly Bean Open Special Bass Tournament. Traffic was backed up from bass boats, being pulled by cars, vans, trucks, and even a team of Amish work horses. Everyone was getting ready for the big tournament.

All the spy squirrels watching Kochi's secret laboratory told me that activity was at a fever pitch. Kochi had to improve his experimental Glug-a-Plug design so it would catch the big bass and win the tournament. In the center of Kochi's laboratory was a monster tank filled with trophy-sized bass. One side of the tank had a built-in big-screen television connected to "Konan," a fifth-generation voice-activated computer, one of the most powerful in the world. Each new lure design was moved across the television screen to get

the reaction of the trophy bass. Konan, the computer, had designed Glug-a-Plug using the latest fuzzy logic and artificial intelligence methodologies.

"Mr. Miyako, logic study show lure to be ninety-nine percent effective in strike performance," the computer spoke.

"You must fix problem. All the fish it catches are same size. Only nine inches long."

"Mr. Miyako, Konan not understand. Doesn't human catching most fish win?"

"No! No! You stupid solid-state reject. Fish must be big. Must catch most big fish to win."

"Please stand by. I'll run a statistical study on Glug-a-Plug's range of effectivity. Done. Study shows that big fish over nine inches in length will strike lure one time for every one thousand casts. Is this satisfactory?"

"No! No! Must continue Glug-a-Plug development until study shows one big bass strike for every cast. Continue, Konan. Hurry. We must win tournament and beat John Lunker Johnson!" shouted Kochi, kicking the bottom of the huge computer console.

"Please watch the bass as I run the Invent-a-Lure software, Mr. Miyako."

The screen image flickered and a new Glug-a-Plug design raced across the screen in front of the hungry bass. Not one moved, not even a flicker or blink of a fish eye. The bass seemed to be in a state of suspended animation. Kochi looked on in shock as example after example of the Glug-a-Plug flashed in front of the watching bass.

The spy squirrels watching Kochi's laboratory knew what was going on with the bass. Kochi held back food from the bass to keep them hungry. The bass had to stage a stop-work action to get fed. Going on "strike" wouldn't work, now would it? Kochi sat staring at the tank, not knowing what to do or how to test the latest development from Konan the Super-Computer. The tournament day was getting closer.

"Kochi, help," squawked Konan's speaker. "Someone from the Internet is trying to hack into the secret disk file for the Glug-a-Plug design."

"Stop them! Give them a fatal virus instead," said Kochi.

"Too late! They got in and are gone now."

"Computer, run design programs all afternoon for new Glug-a-Plug. I must get ready for evening show."

"Show Time for Kochi"

7

Ants and Honey!

It took a lot of courage for Buckshot to go back to Twin Peaks Estates, but Squirrels Forever had to send their very best to spy on Francis and his hoods. Buckshot was gun-shy when it came to AK-47s, so he arrived early in the morning and hid in the attic of the big house, where he could hear everything going on below. It surprised Buckshot when Lunker's girl arrived at the estate for breakfast with Francis.

Millie was wearing her favorite flowered sundress. Her long locks of black hair hung way down her back. Buckshot thought she was beautiful. Francis's mouth dropped open when he saw her step out of the car.

"Hello, Millie. I told you I'd come back for you," said Francis, his eyes traveling from her feet to the top of her head.

"It's been a long time, Francis. Didn't expect to ever see you again. By the size of this place, it looks like you're doing really well."

"Doing fine. Starting a new business and staying out of trouble." Francis chuckled softly. "How about you,

Millie? Still seeing that fish fellow? What was his name? Clunker?"

"Not seeing him anymore, Francis. Plan to get on with my song writing and singing career. I've got a new demo disk the local radio stations are starting to play. Need a chance to get out there and perform," said Millie.

"How about your own country music show, Millie? I'll give it to you for our wedding present," said Francis, slapping his hip and trying to jig.

"Whoa! Slow down, Francis Quantrill. This is the first time I've seen you in years. Don't you think we should get to know each other again first?"

"What do you need to know? I'm rich. I plan to live here in Branson and build a research farm for endangered animals."

"You, Francis? A research farm? said Millie. "A little time here? If you would, Francis?"

"What I'm going to do is good, Millie. No more Chicago family business. Stick around for the meeting this morning with the Indians and you'll see."

Buckshot knew Francis was planning to scalp the Indians. His highfalutin, crooked Chicago lawyers had been working for months and had filed a class action lawsuit for the Indians of Taney County. It was sure to win back one hundred prime acres of land that Francis knew he could steal from the Indians.

When all the Indians arrived at Twin Peaks that morning for the powwow, Francis felt he had them in a barrel and under his control. The old chief Joseph Little Hawk, however, was very leery of Francis. The tribe often had talked about a wildlife protection area, so when Francis promised an endangered species farm, Joseph Little Hawk had listened.

When the meeting started, Bill Fox-Trot, the fishing guide, sat listening and wondering what Francis really was planning. Millie stood with the Indians and looked surprised at what Francis had to say.

Francis spoke of the many species of animals that were now endangered—how man had pushed them from their natural homes, much as the white man had done to the Indians. All the time he was talking, he was chuckling to himself and thinking, 'Extinction ain't all bad. We sure wouldn't want T-Rexes roaming the Ozarks, now would we?'

He finished his talk with a promise to put up the money to build a forty-acre endangered species research park on the land that the Indians would get back from the lawsuit. It would sit right on the edge of The Ozark Fun Land Park. He promised they would have their land soon. As the Indians were leaving, Bill Fox-Trot spoke privately to Francis.

"Quantrill, don't try to go back on your word. We understand the meaning of a gift of dead fishes as well as you do. I hope you understand ants and honey."

"Mr. Fox-Trot. I always keep my word," Francis answered, thinking, 'Here's one Indian who will sleep with the fishes.'

Millie left right after the Indians and headed for Cal and Figgy's house. Buckshot stayed hidden for the afternoon and then raced for town. He was glad to leave the evil house and the attic full of exotic furs and ivory.

It was Red's day to watch Cal Willis's house. So he was there long before Millie arrived, and he found Cal and the three kids having breakfast.

"Figgy, quit fooling with that stupid computer and come have breakfast," Cal yelled.

"Yeah, come on, Mom," said twelve-year-old Jimmie, the oldest of the kids.

"Be there in a minute. Just finishing up our checkbook. You know we could sure use the money if you won the Lilly Bean Tournament, Cal," said Figgy.

"I know, honey. Be fishing with the greatest pro in the country. We gotta win this one. It would be like hitting it big with a country music song."

"I'm surprised you and the pro aren't out scouring the depths of Table Rock Lake this morning," said Figgy.

"Lunker's fish-smelling nose is a little bent out of shape, honey."

"Cal, you ever heard of a Glug-a-Plug?" asked Figgy.

"Nope. Why, honey?"

"Just wondered, that's all. Thought I might do a little fishing too," said Figgy.

"You?" asked Cal, holding back a laugh.

"Yeah, me! You going to help Millie work on that new song idea?"

"Yep, getting the guitar out now. She's supposed to be here any time now," said Cal.

Cal Willis played the guitar like he was born with it in his hands. Red was sure that someday Cal would write a country music hit. Cal was tuned up and ready to play when Millie arrived.

"Hi, Millie!" said Figgy, giving Millie a hug.

"Morning, Figgy. Too bad you missed Lunker's big stage debut at the Opry."

"Yep. Cal said you really pinned the boy's ears to his head," said Figgy. "Good job."

"How you doing, Millie? Ready for a little—'country'? Heard you have a neat hook," said Cal.

"Fishin' hook?" asked Jimmie.

"Nah, It's sort of the heart of a country song," said Millie.

"Well, Jimmie, it's the little catchy phrase every country song has. Finding a good one is like trying to catch lightning in a bottle," said Cal.

"Come on, Cal, let's sit on the back-porch steps and look for some lightning to catch," said Millie.

"Bring him back when you're done with him, Millie," said Figgy.

Cal and Millie sat on the back steps all morning, writing their song, with Cal weaving the chords and rhythms around Millie's words. The song grew from the captured magic of a tiny bit of lightning caught in a bottle. It spoke of a boy and girl in love and building their home on the land where her parents once lived but where today, only a lonely rose bush stands.

There stands a rose.
There stands a rose.
It's all that's left of the passion
and love country folks knew.
It's been twenty-five years
since Mama lived there.
Yet still today...........
There stands a rose.
There stands a rose.

By the end of the morning a new country song was born. This one was going to be a hit. Made Red wish he knew how to dance country. But whoever heard of a dancing squirrel?

When they'd finished, Cal leaned back against the porch railing and stood his guitar on his lap. Millie sat hunched over with her chin on her hands, staring at the yard. As they talked, Cal's fingers never stopped moving on the guitar's neck, as he quietly fingered notes to the melodies that danced in his head.

"Guess this was Lunker's last chance?" Cal asked.

"Oh, Cal. I've played second fiddle to his bass fishing for too long. His missing the wedding was it for me. Shows what comes first for the big hunk. It's the way he is."

"He knows he really screwed up this time."

"Thanks for being both our friends, Cal, but it's over. Like the song said, really over."

"Sorry to hear that, then what's next for you, Millie?"

"Not going to sit around feeling sorry for myself. New opportunities may have just knocked."

"Good luck, gal. Don't forget the dance at the Stag Inn tonight. We're playing and sure would like for you to drop by and sing one for the crowd."

"Figgy!" Millie yelled. "I'm finished with your husband. You can have him back now. Sing one for you tonight, Cal. Think I'll bring a friend."

Millie headed for home, and it was time for Red to head back to squirrel headquarters and find out what Old Buckshot had to say about the bad guys living at Twin Peaks.

8

Dancing The Two Step

All the members of Squirrels Forever were nervous about having a member in danger at the Twin Peaks shooting gallery. So they were glad when Old Buckshot got back safely and slid through the knothole into headquarters. He was tired but wanted to tell them right away about what had happened.

Francis had gotten a call that afternoon from Millie.

"Boss, it's that Millie gal," said Perrino.

"Just give me the phone, stupid," Francis growled. His voice changing to sugar sweet as he addressed Millie. "Hello, Millie. I was spending the afternoon thinking about you in that pretty dress with all the roses—an invitation? When? Tonight? OK. I'll be there in my ten-gallon hat and cowboy boots. Bye." He turned to Perrino, "Get into Branson and buy me a Western outfit. You know, big hat, alligator boots, and all that stupid cowboy stuff."

Red thought about trying to let Lunker know about

this; Francis would be at the dance with Millie, but time was running out and he didn't know how to go about it. It would be about nine o'clock when the dance at the Stag Inn really got going. Nine o'clock is late for squirrels to be out, isn't it? Can you remember seeing squirrels after nine at night? Of course not! They are all fast asleep by that time.

Red and all his squirrel buddies were safely tucked away in their favorite nests when Cal and Figgy dropped the kids off at the mini-golf course next door to the Stag Inn. Figgy had told the kids to crawl in the pickup camper when they got tired. Millie arrived later and joined Figgy at a table down front. Cal and the band had kicked off the evening with a couple of fast two-step numbers and had the crowd up and dancing. Figgy noticed Millie's frequent glances at the front door.

"Looking for Mr. John Lunker Johnson?" she asked.

"Nope, afraid not. He's already here. Sitting alone back in the corner," said Millie. "Asked a friend, Francis Quantrill, to come."

"Wow! That was quick. When did all of this happen? Who's Francis?" asked Figgy, dropping into her chair.

"Francis and I went together in high school. Right up to our senior year. We even talked about getting married. But his family was in some shady businesses in Chicago, and I was never sure I could completely trust him."

"Was that why you broke up?"

"That may have been part of it. About the same time I met a good-looking hunk by the name of John Johnson."

"How'd you two meet, Millie?"

"I was coming out of a football game with the other cheerleaders when he pulled up in his '32 Ford roadster. It was bright yellow, with the top cut off and no fenders. Had a big rumble seat in the back. Said for all of us to climb in. I climbed into the rumble seat and the other two girls got in front. The next time I went for a ride in the roadster, I was in front with John and the rumble seat was empty. Right from the start I should have known. All he talked about was fishing. Couldn't see what was coming for his broad shoulders and good looks. Should have stayed in the rumble seat, Figgy."

"Hey look, Millie, who's that dude with the stupid monster hat with an eagle feather stuck in it?" asked

Figgy, pointing her finger toward the door.

Millie, without looking, answered, "Francis?"

"Well, lucky you! Here he comes," said Figgy.

"Hello, Millie. Who's your friend?" asked Francis.

"Francis Quantrill, meet Figgy Willis. It's her husband's band."

The look on Figgy's face gave away what she was thinking. 'This jerk is as out of place at the Stag Inn as a snowflake at the Alamo.'

"Sit down, Francis and here, let me take your hat," offered Figgy, although she was thinking, 'Love to have two of these ugly things.'

The song ended and Cal stepped to the mike.

"Ladies and gentlemen, your hometown Branson girl is coming up to sing her newest single, A Shooting Star—Make a Wish. Put your hands together for the beautiful Miss Millie Como."

Millie ran to the stage and took the mike with the grace and ease of a star. When she sang, her voice was a sweet blend of old-time country charm and

new-age country rock. The words of her song captured the hearts of all the women in the dance hall.
The men loved her beauty and dreamed of her singing
just to them. Francis listened in astonishment; it was
the first time he had heard Millie sing. He thought,
'I'll make her a big star.' When she finished singing,
the house was on its feet, applauding. John Lunker
Johnson motioned for another tequila.

"Millie, you sing great," said Francis, still clapping his
hands.

"It's about time you got to hear me sing, Francis."

"John's drinking straight tequila," Figgy whispered to
Millie.

"He's probably trying to get the worm out of the bottle to fish with. Come on, Francis, let's two-step," said
Millie.

The closest Francis had ever been to doing a two-step
was tripping as he walked to the dining room table.
Millie was a good teacher; she had a way of floating
on a man's arm like a feather twirling in the wind. She
could make the worst dancer look like he was right at
home on the dance floor. With Francis Quantrill, the
cowboy from downtown Chicago, it wasn't going to be
easy this time. She led him to an empty corner of the

dance floor and pushed him out to arm's length.

"Now, Francis, say after me: Step–Step–Quick–Quick."

"Step–Step–Quick–Quick?"

"That's it; keep saying it and walk toward me. Step–Step–Quick–Quick. Faster, Francis, with the music, with the music. That's it, keep coming toward me. Don't stop saying it, Francis. Step–Step–Quick–Quick. Now lift my hand and let my fingers turn under your hand. No, Francis don't stop. Keep coming as I turn. Keep saying it. Step—OK, you're starting to get it. Keep saying—yeow! Francis! My toe!"

"Can I cut in? I'll try to stay off your lap—I mean, toes," said John Lunker Johnson.

"Go away, Lunker, you're drunk," said Millie.

"Buzz off, bass-breath," said Francis, shoving Lunker back.

"Bass who?" blurred Lunker, grabbing for Francis's shirt.

"Please, John. Don't start trouble. It'll look bad for Cal's band," said Millie.

"Who's this five-and-dime reject cowboy? Looks like the type who would fish with a stick of dynamite," said Lunker.

Millie grabbed Lunker by the arm and dragged him across the floor to his table.

"This is it. Don't do this again. What we had is over. Understand? Fin-n-n-ished. No more second fiddle to you and your bass fishing. Drown yourself in that bottle of tequila, and eat the damn worm. Stay out of my life."

That was enough Stag Inn for one night for Millie. She stomped back to her table to get Francis.

"Where's Francis, Figgy?" asked Millie.

"Said he'd be right back. Here he comes."

"Take me home, Francis."

"What about the two-step, Millie? I was just starting to catch on. Step–Step–Quick–Quick," said Francis.

"Home, Francis. Now! Take me home. Night, Figgy."

"Night, Millie."

As they drove through the Branson 76 Show Strip, Francis thought hard about setting the hook. He was out to catch this sweet dream of a gal.

"Realized tonight how much I had missed you and my old life in the Missouri Ozarks, Millie. Let's go up to my place and have a nightcap. Maybe we can do a slow waltz or two."

Millie didn't answer. She scooted a little closer to Francis and put her head on his shoulder. She felt really alone.

9

The Morning After

While Red scampered along the lakeshore the next morning, he noticed that Lunker's Suburban was still in the parking lot at the Stag Inn. Cal had swiped Lunker's keys when he started drinking, figuring he would sleep the drunk off under a pine tree round back. Red knew Lunker wasn't under the pine tree, because he was watching from there. No one was worried about Lunker...yet!

Chief Little Hawk had called a morning meeting with his tribe to talk about Quantrill's promise to build the endangered species farm. The tribe gathered under a canopy of oak trees on a hill high above the cold, fast-flowing waters coming from the bottom of Table Rock Dam. Some leaned against the trees, others sat in silence, each person seeking his own harmony with the beautiful Ozark Mountains. They heard the wind whisper its hint of freedom through the leaves and branches of the mighty oaks. It carried the scent of distant pine groves and the remembrance of another time when their ancestors lived and hunted—in their time, no one owned Mother Earth. After the bells in the School of the Ozarks chapel chimed to greet the morning, Chief Little Hawk spoke.

"Our bonds with these mountains and the wildlife making their home in them have grown strong. Our white-man neighbors in Branson have proven to be honest and friendly to us and our cause. They have earned our trust and friendship. Who will speak for the outsider that comes to offer protection for the creatures of the forest that are few in number and will soon be lost forever? Who will speak?"

"This man brings promises and much money to carry out his promises. Trust what we see him do. Question the rest," spoke a tribe elder.

"We must see where his true spirit dwells. We must not be surprised by anything he does. The Quantrill family is very powerful and can be very dangerous to deal with," said Bill Fox-Trot.

"We must keep a wary eye on him. We will soon hear, from the courts, about the return of our land. Until our next meeting, may the Great Spirit protect you," said Chief Little Hawk.

About the same time as the tribe was leaving the meeting, Millie left Francis's mansion. She pulled into a Stop-and-Go for gas on the way to Cal and Figgy's. One of the guys in Cal's band pulled up as she waited for the tank to fill.

"Morning, Millie."

"Hi, Jeb. What's up?"

"Wondered why Lunker left his Suburban at the hall last night. Nobody seems to have seen him after the dance," said Jeb.

"Sorry, Jeb. I'm not watching over Lunker any more. It's nice of you to worry about him, though," said Millie.

"You really can't stay mad at the guy, now can you?"

"Sure can, Jeb. He's got his head in the lake most of the time and can't seem to have time for any other life."

"Can't you change him, Millie?"

"I gave up on that, Jeb. Later."

When Millie got to Cal's she found Figgy in the kitchen with the kids.

"Hi, Millie."

"Figgy, Cal around?"

"Cal's been looking for Lunker all morning, Mil. Thought we had him boxed in since we had his truck keys. Can't find him anywhere," said Figgy, with a worried look.

"What's wrong?" asked Jimmie.

"Can't find Lunker this morning, son."

"Mom?" said Jimmie, tugging at her apron.

Cal was pulling up the drive.

"Not now, Jimmie," said Figgy, moving him aside, and stepping onto the porch.

"Hi, Mil. I'm heading up to see if Bill Fox-Trot and the Indians have any news about John. Call me on the cell if you hear anything. Bye," said Cal.

"Good luck, dear," Figgy yelled, as Cal drove out the driveway.

"He's probably out sitting on the bank with a fishing pole," said Millie, shaking her head.

"Come on now, Millie. Still care something for the big lummox, don't you?" asked Figgy.

"Oh, Figgy. If he didn't have such a one-track mind, I could put up with the rest."

"Mom!" said Jimmie.

"What is it, Jimmie?" shouted Figgy.

"Mom."

"I'm sorry, Jimmie, we're worried about Lunker."

"That's what I've been trying to tell you about, Mom. After we finished at the mini-golf last night, we slept in the back of the pickup. Well, Billie woke up; thought he saw something. I didn't tell you right away, 'cause I didn't believe him."

"What? What did he see, Jimmie?"

"He saw two men dragging someone. Honest, Mom, I thought he was fibbin'."

"For goodness sake, Jimmie...was it Lunker? Was it him they were dragging?"

"He didn't know, Mom. He was half-asleep. He didn't

know."

"I've got to call Cal. Right away!" Figgy gasped.

At the end of the day John Lunker Johnson was still missing. Cal had alerted the county sheriff and a full-scale search had been started. The local dive team was called out to explore the lake near the Stag Inn. The Branson police were going house to house, questioning folks for leads. All through the night the search went on. Lunker's fishing buddies showed up with their bass boats; they were crisscrossing the lake, searching the shoreline with spotlights for any sign of John. Lunker was nowhere to be found.

10

The Big Search

The next morning Red watched from his lakeside pine tree as the search teams gathered at the Branson Trout Dock to exchange leads and ideas for the day's search. Everyone was worried but still had a laugh when the Taney brothers showed up, ready to help with their "tracking sow pig." At this point, any help was welcome.

The sheriff divided the county into search areas and sent the assigned teams on their way. The Indian search-and-rescue team headed their pickup trucks and horse trailers toward the rough terrain of the backwoods of Taney County. There had been a report of buzzards circling high above a hilltop.

Millie drove to Twin Peaks Estates to ask Francis to use his helicopter to search for John. Cal headed out for the cliffs and bluffs along the Lake Taneycomo shore.

Out on the lake, the dive team combed the lake bottom but found nothing, except old fishing lures and a couple of tires. No one wanted them to find Lunker that way.

The Taney County sheriff had called for bloodhounds to scent out Lunker's track. Red got the word out early for all the squirrels to stay in the trees so the bloodhounds would have a better chance at picking up Lunker's trail. All the nut-gathering on the ground stopped because of the search. Every squirrel in Taney County headed for the big timber, jumping from tree to tree, searching the ground for John Lunker Johnson.

When Millie got to Twin Peaks, Francis wasn't there. George told her he was flying over Table Rock Lake in the helicopter, studying bald eagles. As she drove back to town she stopped to watch a bass boat skimming the waters of the lake.

She was thinking about the fun she and Lunker had, fishing and riding in Lunker's bass boat. They had been resting in the boat after a swim when Lunker told her how he got his famous name. John and his mom lived by a tree-lined rocky-bottom creek in the Ozarks. His dad left them when John was two, so his mom had to be both parents to him. She was an out-doors girl—didn't like to cook and do laundry—so tak-ing John fishing was right up her alley. She would rig a willow pole with a cork and line and then show him how to push the worm on the hook so it left some big wiggling loops to tease the fish.

"Johnnie," his mom would say, "Swing the line out over a tree limb and lower the worm and cork into the water."

It wasn't long before he started raising and lowering the cork and line.

"Johnnie, you've got to let the cork sit still to catch fish."

John tried to hold the pole still, but something seemed to be telling him, 'Keep the worm moving, Keep the worm moving.' John raised the cork again and again. The big bass hiding in the shade of the tree limb couldn't resist the teasing worm any longer. It charged out from under the limb, gobbled up the worm, and raced for the deep water in the middle of the creek.

"Pull! You got one. Yank him in. It's a lunker, John!"

John swung the bass from the water in one big swoop. It hit him right in the chest. Over he went, with the flapping "lunker" bass in his lap. His mom laughed at the sight of her little boy lying on his back, trying to grab the big fish. That's when John got his famous name. From then on she called him "Lunker." Except when she was mad. Then it was always "John." She never gave her little boy advice on how to fish again; his first fish was bigger than any she had ever caught.

Millie also remembered the key chain John had kidded her with when he got his new boat. On it was written: "Sit Down, Shut up, and Hold On." She couldn't hold back the tears. 'Oh! John, I hope you're alright...'

Meanwhile, up near Rattlesnake Hollow the Taney brothers were being dragged along behind their tracking sow. She was lumbering forward, raising and lowering her nose, smelling the wind and then the ground. Brown foam and slobber was dripping from both sides of her mouth. She was on a hot trail.

"Roy, ain't this the hollow where them other boys are workin' moonshine?" asked Junior.

"Might be, Junior. I see some smoke risin' from up yonder apiece. Do you suppose Mr. Lunker would be up in this here hollow? That wasn't his car parked back there on the road."

"Don't know, Roy. This is where they sent us to look. That car had a big dent in the side of the door."

The bottoms of Junior's shoes were starting to smoke as Roy yelled, "Hold her back some, Junior. I can't keep up."

"I can feel it on the bottom of my foot. She's on a hot track for sure, Roy."

"Let her go, Junior. We can follow her grunts and squeals."

The sow charged ahead, dragging her lead rope. It's fun to watch a pig run. They're not in a hurry very often, except to eat, so they don't get a lot of practice. Squirrels just drop their tails straight behind when they run and go like a hawk is about to grab them. Pigs? Well, it can be called lumbering. Seems the front of the pig doesn't know what the two hams on the rear are doing. Anyway, the sow was in a big hurry, heading up the hollow.

Up ahead a man in a black suit was squatting, peering over a brush pile with his spyglasses at the moonshiners sticking firewood under their still. He was so busy peering that when he stopped to scratch his ears and neck, he didn't hear what was coming up behind him.

The sow had gotten quiet when she spotted him. Now she crept forward, her head lowered, her ears flattened tight against her head. She had the "I've got

She's on a hot track for sure

you now, pig stalker" stare in her beady pig eyes. Lucky for the man, she stepped on a twig as she was about to crunch down on his leg. The ATF agent spun around and went for his holster. The sow head-butted him, shoving him over the brush pile onto his back.

"I'm going to blow that Cujo pig to hell!" he yelled.

At that second the moonshiner saw the revenuer and let go with both barrels of his shotgun. Lead pellets snapped twigs and splattered limbs over the agent's head. He turned, blasting away, emptying his clip before realizing he was hitting the still and not the moonshiners.

The still blew steam from all the new holes and then exploded, spewing flaming moonshine every which way. The agent went pancake flat on the ground! Junior grabbed the sow by the ear and half-dragged her back out of the hollow. The moonshiners tripped over each other as they topped the rise and disappeared. When the burning moonshine fire died down, the agent sat up, took out his "Most Wanted" list, and wrote "pig" at the top.

Miles away, Old Buckshot watched the Indians. It was mid-afternoon. Bill Fox-Trot, on his white-and-black painted pony, led the mounted search team along a spring-fed creek.

When the Indians heard the helicopter dart overhead and hover near the top of the ridge, they thought it was searching for Lunker. They climbed the steep slope out of the valley to get a closer look. The heart-rending sight overhead sickened them.

"Look, the 'copter's right over an eagle's nest!" Bill Fox-Trot yelled.

"The female eagle's sticking tight on the nest," said a rider. "The 'copter's going to blow the nest out of the tree."

"The male eagle's circling in front of the 'copter, trying to lead it away from the nest. Look! The pilot has seen him. He's chasing it! By Geronimo, if I had a rifle I'd shoot the chopper out of the sky!" screamed Bill Fox-Trot.

The Indians watched the brave bird's attempt to stay ahead of the helicopter and lead the devil pilot away from its mate and their high nest. The helicopter was too fast. Climbing above the eagle, the helicopter's plunging downwash blasted the huge bird out of the sky. The eagle fell into the treetops, spinning and bouncing from branch to branch as feathers floated behind, covering the broken limbs. The riders pushed their ponies hard at a gallop toward the trees where the eagle had fallen.

"There's the eagle. He's hurt," said a rider.

"Go to him quickly. We must help him," said Bill Fox-Trot. "He's still alive, maybe just stunned. Cover his head with the backpack to keep him quiet. We must get help for him."

"What kind of man would do this to a bald eagle, the symbol of our country?" asked the rider.

"I've seen that helicopter before. I know what kind of man. The same kind of man that would cheat us out of our land. Take the eagle back; we'll stay and look for John. We'll make camp here for the night," said Bill.

Old Buckshot had watched as the eagle fell and the helicopter dropped out of sight behind the ridge. He knew the eagle was hurt; he also knew the eagle's spirit, how it would someday proudly fly again. The eagle's day would come.

"Got to get out of here!"

11

Really, Really, Bad Luck

Lunker was dazed but awake enough to realize the sun was straight overhead. His face had been buried in something that smelled sickening sweet. It didn't taste too bad until he realized it was bat guano. He was lying on top of a huge mound of it. John shook his head and tried to wipe the guano away from his eyes and mouth. He sat staring at his burning hands thinking, 'How could all this bad luck happen to me? First, missing the wedding, then Millie telling me it's over, and now this!' He knew Francis Quantrill was somehow responsible for his being up to his eyeballs in bat crap.

When he looked up all he could see was a circle of light high above. A sinkhole cave. Around the edges of the deep shaft he could hear the loud clicking of thousands of bats. Their gray color blended with the darkness of the roof and made the walls come alive with a squirming mass of tiny staring eyes. They gave John the creeps. As he started to stand, he stumbled and fell back into the guano. His hand felt for the big knot on the back of his head.

"Got to get out of here!" he yelled.

His voice bounced off the walls—and the bats. The noise from the spooked bats was louder than a hundred witches mounted on their brooms, swooping around his head. John realized that quiet might be better.

The hangover and the knot on his head were hitting him full force. He needed a fire and a torch for light, but everything was spinning. He had to put his head down. Stop the spinning...spinning.

When he awoke he shook his head, trying to clear it so he could see his hands. He thought for a moment that he was blind. A blanket of blackness covered him. The clicking sound of the bats had stopped. They were gone into the moonless night.

The wet cold of the cave made Lunker sit with his arms wrapped around his legs. He remembered stories about a lost sinkhole cave—how people had fallen in and were never found. Wide awake now, John took stock of his pockets—not much—a pocketknife and some change. 'No help here, he thought.' Lunker felt his way around the edges of the sinkhole cavern, pushing aside the logs and brush that had fallen in over the years. He was cold and knew he might never find a way out of the cave.

12

Another Chance at Love

The Indians found the sink-hole cave late that same night.

"You, down there, Lunker?" yelled Bill Fox-Trot from far overhead.

In minutes the Indians had ropes into the cave, and Lunker was on the way to the top. He was cold, bruised, and sore but alive. The team quickly built a fire and covered Lunker with blankets. They would rest and spend the night on the ridge.

"What happened, Lunker?" asked Bill Fox-Trot.

"Not sure. Walked out of the dance, headed for the back of my Suburban to sleep off a nasty drunk. Next thing I knew, woke up in the bottom of this sinkhole. Somebody must have thrown me down there. Somebody wanted me dead. Didn't count on the pile of gua-no breaking my fall," said Lunker.

"Rest. We'll get you back home in the morning," said Bill.

"Thanks, for getting me out of that grave, Bill. You saved my life."

It was high noon when the search team rode into Branson. The entire town had turned out to welcome Lunker back and to thank the Indians for finding him. Cal, Figgy, and Millie waited in the parking lot of the Stag Inn. When Lunker saw Millie he pulled the mule to a stop, jumped off, and walked slowly toward her.

"Tell him. Tell him you still love him, Millie," whispered Figgy.

"I'll try."

Millie didn't have a chance to speak.

"You can have the rich crook and his Twin Peaks mansion, I must be the wrong man for you," Lunker said, as he quickly turned and walked to the Suburban. Millie stood wide-eyed, with both hands on her hips, trying to catch her breath as he drove off.

"What was the stuff all over his face and clothes?" asked Figgy.

"Crap! He so full of it, it's coming out of his ears now," said Millie.

13

Some Serious Fishing

Things got really exciting at Twin Peaks when Francis saw the newspaper headline that Lunker had been found alive. He was so mad he sent George and Perrino to shovel out all the horse stalls in the stable. He sat staring at the newspaper and didn't get over being mad 'til he saw the big ad about the sale over at the Diamond Emporium.

'Diamonds, diamonds, diamonds!' Francis thought. 'I love diamonds. Lots of diamonds for my Millie. We'll see about this big diamond sale. They won't have any diamonds left to sell when my boys get through with them.' He tossed down the paper and called out,"George! Perrino! Where in the hell are those bungling idiots?"

"We're coming, boss," shouted Perrino.

"I'm going to give you both a chance to make up for not getting rid of fish-face. Get some hillbilly clothes and wigs and go get all those diamonds. Do it tomorrow afternoon; that's when all the folks get back to town from The Ozark Fun Land Park. The place will be packed. If you get caught, I don't know you. Understand?"

"Yes, boss. We understand. We'll get them," said George.

All the members of Squirrels Forever were celebrating as the sun went down. Lunker had been found alive. Francis "the Maggot" Quantrill's plan to get rid of Lunker hadn't worked. Still Red knew Lunker was a very unhappy man about now, giving up his last chance to marry Millie. Well, the Lilly Bean Tournament was only four days away, and with any luck at all Lunker would be able to set a world's record for the largest catch of bass in tournament fishing history. Red thought fishing was good for a man's mental outlook on life. Lots better than squirrel hunting. He once heard somewhere that God adds the time a man spends fishing to his allotted days. He was thinking maybe; he should take up fishing—got enough lures to last a while. Might live a lot longer too.

The next morning Lunker and Cal headed out for some serious fishing. Lunker had the bass boat's live wells primed and filled. He was looking for a trophy bass to hang over his fireplace. Fishing had gotten serious. They only had the morning, because John had

"Some serious fishing.?"

promised to meet the Taney brothers at Skunk Creek Cove later in the day to give them some tips and take them up to the big BassPro Shop in Springfield to get some lures.

"Let's make a run up the North Fork, Cal. We won't be fishing that arm during the tournament. It's about eight miles up there; shouldn't take us but seven minutes to get there."

Cal was piloting Lunker's twenty-four-foot metallic painted rocket ship. The 225 hp black monster engine idled softly as Cal ran the electric trim to set the engine full down for take off. They backed slowly away from the dock and idled out past the no-wake buoys. Both turned their cap bills to the rear. Two boys at play!

"Hit it, Cal."

The power surge from the engine was awesome. The front of the boat rose skyward and, in a leap of less than ten feet, came down to slap the water and bring the boat onto plane. The Speedo whooshed past 50 mph as Cal trimmed the engine up for max speed. He huddled behind the tiny windshield as the increasing wind buffeted his glasses and tore at his jacket. Lunker sat looking ahead and smiling. At 85 mph, the front of the boat was sailing; only the back edge and the prop were making contact with the water. The balancing act made Lunker smile even more. Right on the edge of flying. 'Right on the edge of destruction,' thought Cal, as he backed the power off and settled for a smoother 65 mph. It wouldn't do for Cal to hit the water; he couldn't swim.

As the boat entered the north fork arm, Lunker pointed toward the west bank and a rocky point jutting into the water. Cal powered the engine down slowly to keep the tall wave behind the boat from rushing forward and swamping the shallow rear end. When the boat stopped, Lunker climbed onto the front, lifted the trolling motor, and dropped it into position. He took three graphite rods from the rod box and set them just behind his position. Each was rigged with a different type of artificial bait. John selected his favorite, a single-bladed spinner bait with a dark skirt.

"Why the single blade, John?" Cal whispered.

"Water's clear. Don't need as much to attract the ass. They should be feeding up in the shallow water time of morning. If they're slow to hit, I keep ng it back at the same place. The throbbing f the spinner will make El Lunko mad."

an expert with any kind of reel and rod. e could drop the lure on a dinner plate.

He watched as Cal threw his Texas worm rig into the deeper water off the rocky point.

"Good cast. Relax and let it sink. Start it back slowly. Watch the line! Watch the line! It's moving sideways. Hit him, Cal."

Cal had the first bass of the day. Lunker reached over the boat's edge and grabbed the bass by its lower jaw and handed it to Cal. After removing the hook Cal gave the bass a tiny kiss on the forehead and tossed it back into the water.

"Bye, little fellow. Catch you later," said Cal.

"Go back to the same place. Might be another."

"Why did you pick him up by the lip? The dip net is quicker and you don't lose as many if you miss grabbing them," said Cal.

"Better on the fish to pick them up by the lip if you're going to let them go. Dip nets rubs their scales and can cause an infection that can kill them," said Lunker.

"Fishin's getting really technical, isn't it?"

"Wait 'til you see some of the new equipment on t'

boats in the tournament. Guys are using GPS units with contour maps to locate the hot fishing holes. Uses satellites to calculate where the boat is. Has a memory and can take you back to the same place."

"You getting one?"

"Not for a while."

"Lunker, see that swirl?"

"I'm on it."

Lunker's spinner quietly hit four feet on the other side of the still-swirling water. He let the lure drop for five seconds and then brought it up quickly to run right at the surface. Lunker's arm tensioned in antici-pation of the strike. The lure passed the swirling wa-ter; no strike came. Lunker stayed with the lure and brought it toward the boat in a teasing, jerking move-ment. From deep on the bottom, the huge bass turned and accelerated for the lure. The water exploded as the bass smashed the lure. Lunker reared back and buried the hook with a thud. The fight was on.

"Damn, Cal. Look at this. Look at this!"

"Watch him, John. He's heading for the stumps."

"The Macarena."

"Come on, big boy. Get out of there! Feels like the big daddy."

"Work him, Lunker."

"Got to let off on the fighting drag. He's going to break the line, sure as heck. Watch him! He's coming up."

As the big-daddy bass broke through the surface, Lunker wound up the slack line as the bass walked toward the boat on his huge tail, slapping the water into a froth as he came.

"Look at him dancing, Lunker. I think he's trying to do the Macarena."

"Get the net, Cal."

"Net?"

"The net! Now! This guy going to have the privilege of being stuffed and mounted on my mantle. He's close to a record."

"Keep him steady," said Cal.

"That's it. Here he comes."

"Got him. Wow!"

Lunker lifted the huge bass from the net and held him high over his head. After weighing the fish, he dropped it in the live well for the trip back. Lunker had the catch of the day, for sure.

Time to relax and let the boat drift. It didn't take long for the conversation to get around to talking about Millie.

"Before you caught the big daddy I was a little worried about you, the way you looked so downhearted and all," said Cal.

"I'm missing her a lot, Cal."

"You guys been together a long time; had some good times, I bet."

"Sure have. I ever tell you about the time Millie and I drove down to Toledo Bend to bass fish? I had been pushing my luck with the fishing trips—never taking her to a movie or dinner. You know how women get. Well, I was in a rush—unstrapped the boat and had Millie back the trailer into the water. Boat popped off the trailer before I got the engine started. Millie pulled the trailer up on the ramp and watched as I fooled around resetting the kill switch. It was about then I heard the gurgling sound coming from the back of the boat. Realized I had forgot to put the plug in the drain hole. Water was coming in fast.

"Started the bilge pump and asked Millie politely to back the trailer in. She pretended she didn't hear. I was starting to panic but didn't want to let her know I had pulled the stupid trick of leaving the plug out. This time I yelled a little louder for her to back the trailer in. She couldn't pretend she didn't hear this time. Looked at me with a straight face and asked,

'Are you having some sort of crisis, Lunker?'

"Well, that did it! I yelled at her to back the damn trailer in the water 'cause I left the stupid plug out of the back and I was sinking fast. She yelled back for me not to yell at her, and back she came with the truck and trailer. Only problem, she didn't stop backing 'til the water was six inches deep in the truck's cab. She jumped out and left it sitting there. The trailer was clear out of sight. I finally got the boat started and ran the front end up on the bank. Ended up going swimming to get the plug back in and rescue the wet truck. After it was all over, I told her I was sorry for yelling at her. We both had a good laugh. She got to go to three or four movies over that one. We've had some good times, Cal. Wish Francis had stayed in Chicago."

"Figgy would have drowned me and the truck," said Cal. "Don't give up. Go talk to her. Get a bottle of wine and two dozen red roses and go over there tonight."

"You know, I think I will."

14

Stick 'em up!

Meanwhile, the Taneys had stopped in Branson for a "touch of the spirits," as their mom called it. They pulled off the busy street and had a hard time finding a place to park close to the liquor store. The big diamond sale next door was taking up all of the parking. Roy finally found a place for their rusty green Ford pickup next to a large tour bus that was unloading in the parking lot. The bus had just come from The Ozark Fun Land Park, and two of the passengers, Edith and Gladys were really into the Ozark hillbilly fun and ready to shop for their grandkids.

"Oh, look, Edith," said Gladys, spying the Taneys. "It's the hillbillies we saw at the park; who shot at the revenue agents."

"You boys off work for the day? Thought you would've changed clothes when you went home," said Edith.

"Nope. We don't never change our bibs if we can hep

it. It puts our mama in a bad mood if she has to wash 'em," said Junior.

"Aren't they cute, Edith?"

"You boys buying diamonds today?" asked Edith.

"Don't think so. We're lookin' for some Red Dog," said Junior.

"Hope they don't have 'Pig Beer.' Somebody would probably talk Junior into buyin' it," said Roy.

"You boys sure are funny," said Edith, with a big smile.

"Bye now; see you at the next show. Come on, Edith, let's go see what kind of diamond Che-Che is going to buy me," said Gladys.

"Che-Che is your dog, Gladys. How's a dog going to buy you a diamond?" asked Edith.

"Come along, Edith, dear. Teach you a little lesson about surprises. Che-Che gets them for me all the time."

Gladys, you're a stitch."

By now the bus was empty, the Diamond Emporium was full, and Junior and Roy were in the liquor store getting their beer. Neither of them noticed another old green truck pulling in on the other side of the bus.

"Put on that stupid hillbilly hat, George, and let's go get those diamonds," said Perrino.

"You forgot to get some old shoes. Nobody ever saw a hillbilly wearing patent leather shoes," said George.

"I'll rub some dirt on them on the way into the Diamond Emporium. Got your sawed-off shotgun ready?"

The crowd of ladies gave Francis's hoods a round of applause as they entered the crowded store.

"Good show, fellows. Liked your performance."

Perrino and George stared at each other with a look that asked, "What the heck is going on here?" They slid their hillbilly hats down over their faces and walked slowly toward the large display case that contained the diamonds. The ladies went back to shopping and looking at souvenirs and didn't pay any more mind to the two hillbillies—'til George pulled the shotgun.

"OK! Everybody hit the floor! This is a stick-up!" said

George.

"Look, Edith. It's those hillbillies again," said Gladys.

"Don't pay any attention to them, folks. They're really very sweet. Smelled bad, though," said Edith.

"Shut up and give me your purse, lady," said Perrino.

"Here you are, young man. This is really fun! Getting to take part in a show," said Edith.

"This ain't no show, lady. Shoot something, George."

George blew a light fixture and the nearby sprinkler system into shreds. Water sprayed everywhere as Perrino broke the case and stuffed the diamonds into the purse. Folks ran in every direction. George and Perrino ran out the back door toward the truck. They heard the sirens as they raced around the big bus. They didn't know it, but the police were stuck in the traffic, three blocks away, on the busy Branson 76 Show Strip. The door to the bus was open and the bus was empty, so George and Perrino threw their hats under the front of the bus, entered, and ran to the back.

"Quick! Throw the purse out the window and into the truck. Slip off these wet overalls. Good thing we wore our regular clothes underneath. Nobody will recognize us now," said Perrino.

George and Perrino sat slumped in the back seat of the bus. The tour ladies all were standing around in the front of the store, soaking wet, when the police

arrived. No one was sure what had happened; they only knew that two hillbillies had robbed the store and gotten away. It was about the same time that the Taneys came out of the liquor store with their Red Dog beer.

"Brother Roy, look at them new hats layin' under the bus. Let's get 'em. Nobody'll mind."

"Hurry up, Junior. There's funny-lookin' wet ladies walkin' all around back here. Let's git."

George and Perrino watched in surprise as the Taneys got in their truck and drove off.

"Their goes our truck!" said George.

"No, THERE GOES OUR DIAMONDS! That's not our truck. Ours is on the other side. The boss is going to kill us! Head for the car we hid and watch which way they go!" shouted Perrino.

The Taneys headed down a gravel road out of Branson, toward Skunk Creek Cove. Roy was driving, while Junior was on his third Red Dog beer and starting to howl after each sip.

"Roy! I didn't know you carried a purse."

"Ain't my purse, pig-breath. What's in it?" snapped Roy.

"Well, here's an apple. You hungry?"

"I ain't hungry," said Roy. "What else is in the purse?"

"Feels like rocks down here in the bottom. DIA-MONDS! LOTS OF DIAMONDS!" said Junior.

The dust cloud behind the truck kept the Taney

brothers from seeing the ex-cop car until it was too late. The buckshot load from George's sawed-off shotgun sprayed the back of the old truck, knocking out the back window.

"They's shootin' at us!" said Roy.

"Drive faster! They's catchin' up to us and tryin' to pass. Looks like the cops!"

"They don't look like no cops I ever saw 'round here. It's an old Branson Dodge cop car," said Roy.

"Run them in the ditch, Roy."

"Hang on. They're gonna ram us."

The front of the ex-cop car was no match for the steel of the Taneys' old pickup bumper and trailer hitch. The plastic grill of the car crumbled as the trailer hitch punched a big hole in the radiator. Steam and water poured out. The temperature gauge on the big V-8 was headed for the danger zone.

"Roy?"

"Wha-at? What you want, Junior?"

"Wonder if that's where they got the name for the

Dodge Ram."

"Shut up. Climb through the window, Junior. Roll a couple barrels of moonshine at 'em."

"Ain't gonna waste good whiskey."

"Can't drink it if we's dead," said Roy.

Junior's first barrel hit the road right in front of the big V-8. When it busted open, it sprayed the radiator and the hot engine and then spurted on the hot exhaust pipes.

"Hurry, Junior, we don't have far to go before we get to the boat dock. I'll slow up a little. See if you can put a barrel right on top of their hood."

"I got 'em. I got 'em, Roy," said Junior, lifting the barrel over his head.

The second barrel smashed into the hood, cracking the windshield and soaking the car from top to bottom. The heat from the engine and exhaust pipes ignited the one-hundred-proof moonshine. The car was a ball of dust, steam, and flames. It was quite a sight for the guys fishing around the dock, as the flaming car roared through the last stretch of woods and fireballed off the high cliff into the water. Some of the fishermen thought a comet had hit the lake! Roy and Junior pulled up in the parking lot at the dock and sat there, staring at the huge waves that hit the dock.

"What happened to those guys shootin' at us, brother Roy?"

"Don't know. Get rid of the purse, Junior. Dump the diamonds in the fishin' tackle box. Come on, let's get to the boat before somebody else shoots at us."

The Taneys hurried down the dock and tossed the tackle box onto their boat.

"Junior! Look at the boat deck. I told you not to leave that sow pig tied on here all mornin'. She still ain't housebroke."

"Look at all the foam comin' out of her mouth. She's mad. Somebody must have tried to steal our boat. Come here, nice piggie, piggie," said Junior, rubbing the sow's dripping snout.

As the boys pushed away from the dock, one of the guys who was fishing in a bright-green bass boat yelled, "You ought to keep that pig home. Some guy walked by and she tried to take his leg off."

With the rose pink sow standing at the bow,
her snoot lifted high sniffing the wind; the
canoe boat turned majestically away from
the dock and chugged across the lake.

"Did he have black pants on?"

"Sure did."

"She must have thought it was that revenue fellow," said Junior.

"Head across the lake. We gotta find Lunker. He'll know what to do about the diamonds," said Roy.

With the rose-pink sow standing at the bow, her snout lifted high, sniffing the wind, the canoe boat turned majestically away from the dock and chugged across the lake.

"Slow down, Junior. New motor pushin' us near 'nuff at breakneck speed. Bailin' wire startin' to come apart on some of them canoes. Besides, my new hat almost blew off when she came up on the plane."

As inventions go, the canoe boat was a doozy. Each time out it handled differently. Each one of the eight old, bent-up, aluminum canoes had a way of thinking for itself. As the boat rode the waves, the bailing wire would stretch and strain as each canoe tried to go its separate way. Only lady luck held the whole mess together. Anyway, today was lucky for the Taneys; she was holding together. Not far behind them, the bright-green bass boat was coming up fast.

"Look! The fishin' fellow in the green boat is chasin' us," said Junior.

"Ain't him. It's them. The two fellows who was in the Dodge Ram car."

"We can't outrun them this time, Roy. We'd better stop and see what they want."

The stolen bass boat circled the Taneys' canoe boat, as Roy, Junior, and the sow pig stood watching. As the boat pulled along side the canoe boat, Junior heard the sow pig's deep growl.

"You dumb hillbillies nearly killed us back there," said Perrino.

"Why you go shootin' at us?" asked Junior, holding the sow tight by the collar.

"Shut up and hand over our diamonds. We found the purse back there at the dock. So we know you got them," said Perrino.

"Roy, the sow pig is growlin' real bad," whispered Junior.

"I know. They both got on black pants," whispered Roy.

"What are you two whispering about? Shut up, before I shoot you both," said George.

"We was just sayin' our sow pig really likes your boat," said Roy.

The sow had flattened her ears and was just waiting for someone to say the magic words: "Sic 'em."

With a kick from Roy, the sow dove into the middle of the green bass boat. Perrino and George had never faced a mad pig before, so surprise turned to fright as she charged Perrino.

It was a sight that belonged in a movie—the sow snorting and hawing, with foam and froth dripping from her mouth, heading right for the center of Perrino's pants. Perrino turned white as a ghost and yelled for George to shoot the demon pig. George lit off the shotgun twice toward the pig, but the shots went way wide as the boat rolled on a wave. They ripped up the bottom of the boat, and a fountain of water lifted into the air. Perrino jumped to save his manhood, and the sow turned toward George, who was trying to reload the double-barrel.

"I'll get you this time!" he yelled.

Guess poor old George plum forgot about Junior and

Roy. Junior wasn't going to let anybody shoot his tracking pig. He was swinging the canoe boat's anchor in a great arc when it hit George in the middle of his back. It was about that same time that the sow pig sunk her teeth into George's right leg.

"Call the pig off, quick, Junior. There's a sheriff's water patrol boat coming across the lake now. We got to get out of here."

With the pig back on the canoe boat, the boys sped on to find Lunker. Behind them, Perrino was dog-paddling and cussing up a blue streak, while poor George sat holding his bleeding leg. That was the way the sheriff's deputy found them.

Two miles down the lake the Taneys met up with Cal and Lunker. Cal had the radio on, listening to the reports of the big diamond heist in Branson.

"Howdy, boys. Come out to get some fishin' tips?" asked Cal.

"Mr. Lunker, you got to help us. The sheriff's boat is right behind us. They's gonna thunk we stole them there diamonds. We didn't steal nothin', 'cept a bottle of wine Junior stuck in his drawers at the liquor store," said Roy.

"What do you mean? You boys got those diamonds?" asked Lunker.

"They's in this here fishing tackle box. We took 'em out of a purse and stuck 'em in with our baits," said Junior.

"Give me the box—quick," said Lunker.

Lunker opened the tackle box to find it crawling with live bait. But as he lifted the worms, he saw the whole corner of the box was filled with beautiful stones.

"Holy jumping bullfrogs! They're here! Quick, Cal. Give me the bass out of the live well."

Cal held the big bass as Lunker quickly stuffed two handfuls of diamonds down the fish's throat. Cal dropped the bass back into the live well and picked up his fishing rod as the sheriff's boat pulled alongside. The bass was splashing around in the live well when the red-headed deputy sheriff stepped on board Lunker's boat.

"Well, hello again, John Lunker Johnson."

"Hello yourself, Judy Campbell."

"We had a little excitement in Branson this after-

"The Diamond Bass of Table Rock Lake"

noon. Those two fellows sitting handcuffed in the back of my boat said they saw the two hillbillies who stole the diamonds, and they're sitting there next to your boat," said Judy Campbell. "They look like the Taney brothers to me."

"We've been fishing out here all morning," said Lunker. "Taneys promised to come out and join us, for some fishing tips."

"Why don't all you fellows line up on the side of the boat? Afraid I'm going to have to frisk you."

As Lunker leaned forward against the side of the boat, Judy began a long, slow pat down, starting at the ankles and ending at the back of his head.

"Well, wasn't that nice? See what you've been missing?" asked Judy.

"My life's been sort of a wreck lately. Sorry, Judy."

"Well, is that so? What's that splashing around in the live well?"

"It's a lunker bass to put over my fireplace."

Judy opened the live well door and lifted the bass from the water.

"Wow! Heavy fellow, isn't he? Bet he would like for you to practice catch and release, Lunker. Whoops! Sorry! He slipped right out of my hands."

The big bass was thrashing to swim, even before it hit the water. It dove quickly out of sight, as Lunker and Cal watched the spreading ripples in disbelief.

"All you people get in my boat. We're going downtown for a lineup. You and Cal can go on fishing, Lunker. See you tonight," said Judy, as she winked at Lunker.

As the boats pulled away, Cal and Lunker stared into the water where they had last seen the diamond-filled bass.

"Did you see that? She just tossed the richest bass in the world back in the lake, Cal."

"Start casting," Cal said dryly.

"Word gets out about this; everybody in the country will be coming to Branson, trying to catch the diamond bass," said Lunker.

"How long has Judy been trying to catch you?" asked Cal.

"She's only testing the waters."

"Sounds like she wants to go swimming."

"If the roses and wine work, I might be swimming with Millie tonight."

"Good luck, Lunker."

"Cal, I need a big favor. Just this time, buddy?"

"You want me to call her for you?" asked Cal, a frown crossing his face.

"Sure do. I won't mess up this time. OK?"

"This is it, good friend. One time."

"Thanks, Cal. Tell her I'll be over at eight sharp," said Lunker.

"Don't forget the roses."

"I won't."

Cal and Lunker decided they'd had enough of the most expensive fishing trip they had ever been on, so they stowed their fishing rods, folded the bass boat seats, and headed for town. Meanwhile, the sheriff's office was busy trying to sort out the real diamond thieves. With no evidence to go on, Judy Campbell finally had to let all four of the suspects go. The Taneys headed for home. Perrino and George stopped by Dick's Five & Dime Store in downtown Branson to buy some heavy work gloves. Francis would put them to work shoveling horse poop when he heard about the lost diamonds.

15

Red Roses and Wine

Lunker pulled into his driveway, got out, and raced into his house. He swept everything to the side in his refrigerator and placed the two dozen, personally selected, deep-red roses on the bottom shelf; then he headed for the shower. He paused long enough to glance in the mirror. The sight of his long shaggy hair surprised him. Heck, it only been two...four...six months. Lunker raced back out the door and headed for a haircut.

"Hi, Margie. Tina in?"

"She's in the back. Tina! Got a customer out here."

"Who's out there?" asked a voice from behind the door.

"It's Lunker—he looks likes a shaggy dog."

"Go ahead, sit down; be right there," said Tina.

Lunker always liked to talk fishing with Tina. You see, Tina was an avid walleye fan, and every chance she got was spent dragging the bottom of the lake after the elusive fish. Tina liked to tease Lunker about fishing only for bass and then never eating them.

"Where you been, big boy? You sure look ragged. Millie been cutting on your hair?"

"Haven't been seeing her. Screwed up and missed my own wedding. Can't believe you haven't heard. Thought you heard everything first in here."

"I do. You looked so worn out; thought you might want to talk about it if I mentioned it first. You getting along OK by yourself?"

"Miss her bad. Spent the other night watching her dance with another man. Got on a mighty bad drunk over that."

"Heard you were sort of lost for a couple days," said Tina.

"Felt like I had lost my life mate. Reminded me of an old coyote I saw once. It was raining hard, headlights caught sight of him sitting there on the edge of the road with his ears down flat against his head. Didn't move; just stayed there as I drove by. Came back about an hour later and he was still there, pacing up and down the edge of the field. Looked so sad and strange, I made up my mind to go back out there in the morning. Found out why the coyote was hanging around that spot in the road. His mate had been hit by a car and was lying dead in the ditch. Guess I feel a lot like that old coyote, Tina. Millie said it was over for her. But I can't give up yet. One last chance tonight. Roses and wine. Hope she'll listen."

"She'll listen. You're one of the good old boys, John Lunker Johnson. How's that look? Short enough?"

"Fine. Thanks, Tina. Wish me luck."

Lunker headed for home and the long overdue shower. First, he called Cal to be sure his date with Millie actually was going to happen. Cal teased and said, "No way, man," but then told him the truth. His date with Millie was on. After the shower Lunker shaved quickly with his electric razor and ran his hand over his chin. It was way too rough. Out came the shaving cream and the safety razor. This time the results were better and passed his inspection. The blow-dryer made fast work of his new haircut, as it fell quickly into place.

Picking out the shirt for the evening took the longest time. It had to be just the right color to set the mood. Lunker pushed all the red shirts to the back of the rack and went slowly through the Western blues, finally selecting one that looked like it didn't need to be ironed. After going through all his jeans, he finally found a pair without white accents for his knees. This was the outfit for tonight. Lunker always felt confident in casual clothes. Millie liked him dressed that way too.

Lunker was getting nervous, so he called Cal again to verify the time for his date. Cal told him to relax; it wasn't until eight o'clock. Lunker was ready at seven-thirty. He got the roses and the bottle of California wine from the refrigerator and headed for the front door. He jerked his hand from the doorknob as he heard the soft knock on the other side. When he opened the door, Judy Campbell's tall figure, in a knock-out floor-length dress, was outlined by the sunset.

"Flowers and wine. Thank you, Johnny boy."

"Judy!"

"Aren't you going to ask me in?"

"Oh! I'm sorry. Come in, Judy. I've going to have to run in a couple of minutes. I've got a last chance to see Millie. Sort of a reprieve, I guess."

"You know, there's no reason to chase after a woman who has a rich man in her sights."

"Quantrill?"

"What's with all the aftershave?"

"I'm sorry, Judy. Got to go. Millie's going to be waiting."

"Come on...relax. I'm not going to bite you," Judy said, as she slipped behind Lunker and wrapped her arms around his waist."

Lunker reached behind with his free arm to gently push Judy away. She was waiting for his arm, and Lunker didn't realize she had slipped the handcuff on his wrist until Judy spun him around and he found out they were cuffed together.

"Relax, Lunker. Enjoy the evening with someone who likes you a lot. Enough to kidnap you for herself."

"I can't do this, Judy. I've got to go!" said Lunker, pulling at the handcuff.

"At least share a little of the wine with me," Judy said, as she pulled Lunker down on the sofa.

"Told you I've got to meet Millie in just a few minutes. This is kidnapping, Judy!"

"Never had a man complain about it before. Open the wine, Lunker."

"Promise, you'll let me out of these handcuffs if I do."

"Sure, hon."

Lunker opened the wine and passed the bottle to Judy. She took a long swig from the cold bottle and passed it back to Lunker. Then she turned, draped herself across Lunker's lap, and popped open the snaps on his shirt.

"Ooh! Love the sandy hair on your chest."

"Judy! Will you stop? Please?"

"What's the matter? Can't stand the torture?"

Judy reached for Lunker's head and pulled it toward her face. She kissed him deeply. Lunker was pushing her away when the front door burst open.

"You OK, Lunker?" shouted Millie Como.

"OH CRAP—Millie! I can explain."

"Don't bother, Johnson. It's my time to explain. Cal said for me to meet you here at eight o'clock. I saw the sheriff's car in front and thought you might be in trouble. Looks like I was right again. Deep in trouble." Millie turned and walked out the door.

"Wait, Millie! Give me a chance to explain. Judy surprised me as I was leaving with the flowers and wine for your house. Slipped the cuffs on me when I wasn't looking. See?"

"Cuffs? I don't see any cuffs, John."

"Damn it, Judy! She took them off. Show her the cuffs, Judy!"

"Sorry, Millie. Must be the wine. Gone to his head," said Judy.

"He's all yours, Judy. Hope you can put up with all his crap."

"Millie..."

"Good-bye, Lunker," said Millie, as she slammed the front door behind her.

"Hand me that bottle of wine, Judy," said Lunker.

"Sure. I think we should lock the front door. Don't you?"

"Not tonight, Judy. You know, the big tournament's coming up real soon. Going to need my rest," said Lunker, knowing that things for him and Millie just got a whole lot worse.

"Not tonight, Judy."

16

Big Lilly Bean Tournament

Well, the day of the Big Lilly Bean Bass Tournament had finally arrived. The tiny sliver of the sun breaking over the Ozark Mountains made the cloud of fog covering the starting cove look like a puffy white blanket. It was a happy day for Red and his buddies, all the squirrel hunters had fishing poles in their hands instead of guns. It was hard to find an empty limb in any tree—squirrels had come from miles around to watch John Lunker Johnson become the most famous bass fisherman in the world. Down the bank, people were pushing and shoving, trying to get a place to toss a line in and try for the big bass with all the diamonds tucked inside. The secret had gotten out!

Gurgling engines idled on the water, waiting for the starter's gun to sound. Red and Buckshot were naming the boats they could see. They spotted the Star of Texas first—Kochi's shiny glitter jacket made it easy to see. Kochi was ready with the very latest edition of the Glug-a-Plug, the best-tested lure in history. Then Red spotted his buddy Lunker; Cal was there too. They were getting their gear laid out and tied down for the race up the lake. Buckshot swore he could smell the Taney brothers and their tracking sow pig. Buckshot's eyes were getting old and tired, so Red was the first to see the canoe boat and its new coat of camouflage paint. Roy and Junior had all their bait jars lined up in a row, ready to change baits if the bass were being finicky. Their sow pig was curled, up eyeing the crawdads, hoping that one would crawl out for her breakfast snack.

The fog was still too thick for Red to clearly see the bass boat with the two good-looking gals who were getting ready to fish. Figgy and Millie had been planning for days to surprise Lunker and Cal by entering the tournament and catching the most bass with the new special lure that Figgy got by hacking into Kochi's super-computer. Millie wasn't sure the lure would work—after all, it came from the Internet.

A male bald eagle circled high overhead, its piercing eyes catching glimpses of the boats and water as the fog started to clear. Below, Francis Quantrill stood on the front deck of his luxury liner, peering through a high-power telescope at the idling boats, trying to sort out Fish-bait Lunker. Francis and his crew of pirates were waiting for a chance to ruin Lunker's run at the world's record for bass fishing.

John Lunker Johnson knew this was it—his big chance. Get that twenty-four pounds of fish in the boat, and he would be known as the greatest bass fisherman in the world. He could picture a big movie contract and, for sure, the weekly TV sportsman show he would host. At that moment, Lunker had only one thing on his mind, and it wasn't a woman. Even his friends wondered if the bass fishing title would mean more to him than having Millie Como as his wife.

The starter stepped out on the dock and raised his gun in the air. All the squirrels raced to the backside of their trees to hide. The gun sounded, and the roar of the engines rolled over the water and up the bank, making people gape at the spectacle of the boats competing for the lead positions. Lunker and Cal got a good start but weren't in front. Two high-powered twin-engine racing boats led the pack, their turbo engines making so much noise there wouldn't be a fish within a mile of them when they stopped.

The Taneys were the last to leave the cove. Junior thought the waves must be at least as high as on the ocean. Their canoe boat pitched and rolled, spilling the crawdads across the front of the deck. That was all the tracking sow pig needed—up she sprang, sucking up the crawling crawdads as she scooted across the deck, stomping and jumping on the critters. The waves had broken most of the rusty wire that held the canoes together, and with a final snap, four canoes headed east; the other four went west. Junior was on the eastbound express with the engine, and Roy was westbound, going nowhere. The sow dog-paddled for the bank. She had just plain missed the boat.

Lunker and Cal were still several boats back from the front. The boat that they had noticed following them during early practice was headed right into Lunker's number-one choice spot.

"So that's the scumbag who's been spying on us all last week," said Cal.

"Well, let him have the spot. He won't know about the water color change that happened with yesterday's rain," said Lunker. "We can come back later and hit it with the bright-yellow spinners; should bring 'em up."

In the spirit of good sportsmanship, Lunker and Cal headed for their number-two spot.

They had picked it because it set on the east side of the lake and today the wind was blowing right toward it. It would drive the bait fish right over the rocky point that extended under water, out more than two hundred feet from the bank. Cal had slowed the boat and cut the engine far enough out that it didn't cause the fish to leave their feeding grounds. Lunker pivoted the trolling motor into the water and turned it on high to get the boat quickly positioned to move along the rocky point. Lunker's lure was in the air, riding with the wind, before Cal had a chance to pick up his rod. The spinner hit, dropped, and came back to hit the surface within a couple of feet, and then settled back to ride just under the water, causing a big ridge to rise above it. It didn't get five feet more before Numero Uno nailed it. Lunker had a heavy pull on the lure and only needed a quick snap to set the hook. The bass headed for the deep water, and the reel's drag was letting line out faster that Lunker could reel it in.

"Tighten up, Lunk!" Cal yelled. "He's pulling like a real keeper."

"Caught me a little off guard and not quite ready with the gear," Lunker replied.

Lunker held the surging rod in his left hand and cranked down on the drag to just above the line's breaking point. It was enough to turn the bass and get him headed toward the boat. Lunker swiftly moved him to the top; then he kneeled to reach over the boat's edge to grip the bass's lower lip and lifted him from the water. Cal had the scale and got a quick measurement of five pounds, four ounces. The bass was headed for the already-circulating live well.

The next two spots they tried brought up three Kentucky bass, each under the fifteen-inch length limit. Cal wanted one more cast into the feeding bass. It brought him his first keeper, a nice seventeen-inch "Ken-tuck" that had ripped into Cal's deeper-running lure.

Lunker needed to score again; he folded the trolling motor as Cal dropped his bass in the second live well. It was still early, and Lunker was sure they would find the bass moving from the shallow water back to the deeper water they liked when the sun was up. Cal kicked the big Mercury engine down for the take off and pulled the trigger on it. The nose of the boat sprang off the water and slapped down in an instant, rocketing forward with the boat flying on the back edge of the hull. The boat was making a sweet tap-tap sound as it danced along the top of the lake swells.

"Ain't it sweet?" asked Cal.

"Sure is, Pap," Lunker replied.

Lunker pointed out the cove he had been thinking about, and Cal steered the boat along the bank without going deeper into its entrance. Lunker would set the powerful trolling motor for that. Running quiet was the ticket, even if it took longer.

Halfway back in the cove, Lunker's second cast got the result he was after. Again, the spinner bait had done its work for him. The bass headed for the surface, breaking and dancing across the water on its big wide tail. John had made the set, so the dance did little to shake the treble hook in its mouth. The bass was way beyond a keeper, weighing in at six pounds, eight ounces. A nice catch for any day of the week, let alone a record-setting tournament attempt. Cal noted the weight and calculated that Lunker would need twelve pounds, four ounces to set the record. A mighty big order, but Lunker was tested and true. Cal was sure he could do it.

"Look John, I'm not going to fish; I'll just help you from here on. Tell me what you need and you've got it," said Cal.

"Keep that rod casting, Cal. We got a couple hours yet, and I've still got half a dozen places to cover before we head back for the check in."

Another hour, and the bass had all but turned off for the morning. Lunker would have to get out all the old tricks he could remember for this time of day. Finally, an old fashion Texas worm rig brought in two more fish that were both nice keepers. Cal anxiously ran the total and found that it would take one more fish for Lunker to set the record. Just four more pounds in the boat would do it. Time was getting short.

"John, we need to head back up the lake and get near the weigh-in point," said Cal.

"I know. I'm pulling in. Let's drop the hammer and head for the starting cove," said Lunker.

Lunker had less than fifteen minutes before weigh-in when Cal slowed the boat near the big luxury liner at anchor in the bay. Cal thought it would be a good place to find Lunker's last bass, hiding in the shade of the big boat. Neither of them saw Francis Quantrill leaning over the bow of the boat and tossing buckets full of shiny minnows in the water to draw the bass away from Lunker's boat.

"Having any luck, fish-brains?" Francis yelled. "Too bad you didn't die it that cave. Maybe next time you won't be so lucky."

Lunker didn't answer. He was too busy. He had to catch one more bass. In less than ten minutes he and Cal would have to race for the dock for the take-out and weigh-in.

"One more cast and we've got to motor, my friend," said Lunker. "Don't think I'm going to make it."

"Don't give up guy. Remember that trick your mother taught you. Now's the time to spit on the lure," said Cal.

Lunker lifted the lure to his lips, kissed its nose, and spit right on the top of it.

"Here goes my last chance at the world's record."

The lure hit the water and Lunker watched as it dropped out of sight. Like a freight train headed up the track, the last bass Lunker needed to win, sped from the lake's gravel bottom and sucked in the falling lure. Lunker felt the bass hit and reared back hard to set the hook.

"That's it, Cal. He's on. He's on!"

"Don't rush him, John; holy mackerel, it's a good one."

John had the winning bass hooked solid. The bass bowed the rod tip as Lunker worked him up out of the deep water and toward the side of the boat.

High above the luxury liner, the eagle that had been

circling, waiting for just the right time, folded its wings to its side, and with the speed of an arrow, plummeted toward the man leaning over the edge of the liner. Francis didn't see or hear the arrow strike coming. He went over the rail like a sailor being keel-hauled on a pirate ship. Old Buckshot saw the eagle strike—he jumped up and down, barking in delight, as Francis headed for the water and disappeared below the surface. The watching Indians knew the eagle's day finally had arrived. Francis was paying for his evil deeds. Lunker and Cal were close to the liner and heard the loud splash but didn't realize what it was until Francis came thrashing back to the surface.

"Help! I can't swim!" he yelled.

"Good! Hope you drown!" yelled Lunker, as he worked the bass closer to the boat.

Francis went down again, and Lunker took his eyes off the fighting bass to look at Cal.

"Don't do it, John. Let the S.O.B. drown," said Cal.

"Cal, take the rod. Land him; he's yours. I'm going after the jerk," said Lunker.

Everyone watched as Lunker gave his last-chance bass to Cal and dove over the front of the boat, racing to the spot where he had last seen Francis. He jack-knifed under and grabbed Francis by the hair, pulling him to the surface and swimming, with Francis in tow, to the boat. Cal reached over the side and heaved the choking, coughing Francis into the safety of their boat.

Millie had watched as Lunker dove to save Francis, but she didn't know what Lunker had given up to save the crook.

"Did you see that, Figgy? I can't believe I did!" said Millie. "He put down his damn fishing pole to save Francis. Maybe he's not so bad after all."

At the weigh-in, Cal told Millie exactly what Lunker had given up when he handed over the rod with the record setting bass hooked for the catch.

"You can't be serious. John Lunker Johnson gave up the last bass he needed to win the world's bass-fishing record?" questioned Millie.

"Look at me, Millie. Have I ever lied to you?" asked Cal.

"He did that to save somebody he hated?"

"Yes," said Cal.

He had won a lifetime with the girl of his dreams.

"By gosh, I'm going to marry that man if he'll still have me," she said.

"Oh! He'll have you. Loved you all along," said Cal.

Millie wanted to be near John "Lunker" Johnson, and in the safety of his arms. Lunker was going to win after all. Oh, not the tournament. He had won a lifetime with the girl of his dreams.

17

The Winners and Losers

Old Buckshot and me—we still felt like there needed to be a bit of setting things right. The Indians
thought so too, and the rest of the justice came when
the AFT agents got a tip about Francis's exotic animal
collection. The agents caught him as he was heading
down the path to the waiting helicopter, which was
loaded with poached ivory. Francis was going away for
a long time.

I bet you want to know who won the tournament. It
was Kochi, with his new Super-Glug-a-Plug. He took
home the big Lilly Bean prize and became the most
famous bass fisherman in Branson. Figgy didn't do
very well with her Internet-hacked Glug-a-Plug design. The fish she caught were all the same size and
too small to count. Strange!

And the big bass with the diamonds—whatever happened to him? All of us squirrels still watch the
water's edge, hoping to see him again. He's still out

there in Table Rock Lake, waiting for just the right lure to hit the water. Folks keep coming to Branson to see great country music shows and to try to catch the diamond bass. I keep hanging over the limb of that old tree, and every once in while I steal another bright and shiny fishing lure. With everyone fishing for the bass, no one has time to hunt squirrels. I'd better go now; fall's here and I've got a lot of nuts to gather before winter.

The Diamond Bass is out there—just waiting for you to catch him.